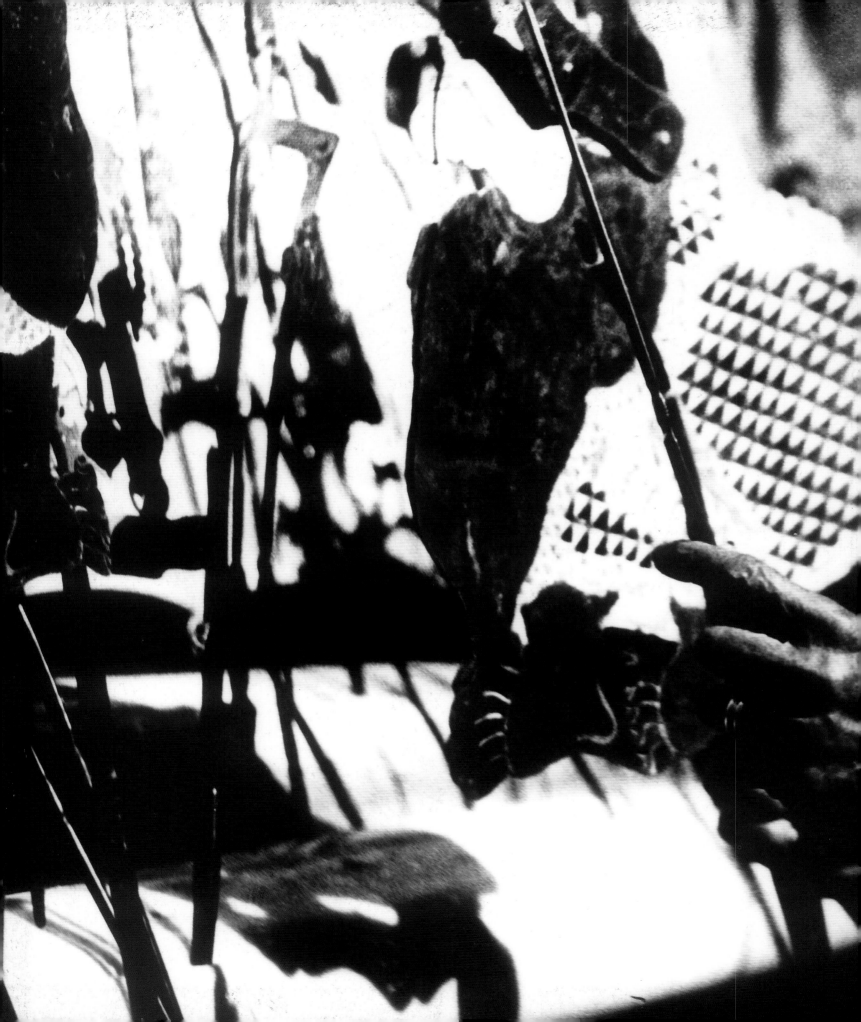

ALIT DJAJASOEBRATA

SHADOW THEATRE IN JAVA

THE PUPPETS, PERFORMANCE AND REPERTOIRE

Published in association with
THE MUSEUM OF ETHNOLOGY ROTTERDAM

THE PEPIN PRESS

AMSTERDAM AND SINGAPORE

ISBN 90 5496 034 5 (hardcover edition)
ISBN 90 5496 052 3 (softcover edition)

A catalogue record for this book is available from the publishers
and from the Royal Dutch Library, The Hague

This book is edited, designed and produced by
The Pepin Press in Amsterdam and Kuala Lumpur
Design: Pepin van Roojen and Dorine van den Beukel
Translation: Robert Lankamp and Andrew May
Copy editing: Andrew May
Photography: Wouter Thorn-Leeson

Textual assistance from Mr R.S. Wassing gratefully acknowledged

The Pepin Press
P.O. Box 10349
1001 EH Amsterdam
The Netherlands
Fax (+) 31 20 4201152
Email: mail@pepinpress.com

Printed and bound in Singapore

Front cover: King Yudistirà, detail of the puppet on page 135
Back cover: Wayang performance, Java
Page 1: Profile of the *gunungan* on page 62
Page 2/3: A dalang from Cirebon in action, 1974

Contents

Foreword

This publication is the climax of a period of almost forty years of systematic and devoted collecting.

The ideas behind this book took shape in 1966, when the exhibition *Wayang purwå; shadow theatre and world view in Java* was shown at the Rotterdam Museum of Ethnology. The young curators responsible for the exhibition, Ms. Alit M.L.R. Djajasoebrata (Curator Indonesia Department) and her colleague René S. Wassing considered it a labour of love. They were (and still are) convinced that 'in wayang resides the soul of Java'. Many rare and beautiful specimens have been added to the museum's rich collection since then.

Alit Djajasoebrata wishes to express her special gratitude to the following persons who so generously shared their insights in this field with her: Armand de Guémenée, K.R.T. Hardjonagoro, Mas Diarto, Prof. Dr. C. Hooykaas, Bernard Surjabrata, Prof. Dr. Benedict O'G. Anderson. Traditional Javanese wayang theatre is a splendid and fascinating world. This book aims to make its many aspects available to a wider audience around the world.

Hein Reedijk
Director
Museum of Ethnology, Rotterdam

Left: Wayang kulit performance in Blora, 1862.

Introduction

Wayang is highly integrated in Javanese society, and many consider it to be a highlight of Javanese culture. Over the centuries, the ancient wayang theatre, with its more religious character, has increasingly developed into a distinct art form; foreign influences introduced new stories, characters were added, and new refined styles were developed at the courts. In the 20th century, wayang theatre has been used to serve political ends.

This book will focus on the most popular form of wayang, which uses flat leather puppets and is based on the *purwå* repertoire. These are ancient stories in which ideas about cosmic events and divine will are represented, and the course of events is seen as being predestined, a part of a cosmic law. Some people even believe that wayang performances have protective powers, and certain plays are thought to chase away evil spells.

Because of the moral dilemmas dealt with by the protagonists, whose actions serve as examples of good and bad behaviour, wayang purwå can also be seen as a way of teaching people the difference between right and wrong. As well as this didactic role, wayang has always been an outlet for opinions, a means of expressing thoughts that could not be said openly. Wayang characters are thus mouthpieces; voices that express disapproval.

This book is an introduction to wayang purwå, describing the origins of wayang, the various types of wayang, and the various characters featuring in the plays. Most importantly, it will describe the main wayang purwå stories which still survive in Javanese society today.

Most puppets in this book are from the collection of the Rotterdam Museum of Ethnology; a few exceptions come from a private collection. The selection is primarily based on aesthetic qualities and the rarity of the puppets.

Left: Wayang kulit performance, Java, c. 1910.

9

Wayang

Javanese children are introduced to wayang at an early age. They see the heroes about whom they have heard stories appear on stage, and slowly they become more familiar with the colourful mix of the various protagonists depicting moral dilemmas. Children sometimes attend performances that last an entire night. The audience is not expected to sit silently at performances: people meet friends and talk to them, look around, and sometimes they get a snack from a stall. People who need a rest take a nap. From experience everyone more or less knows how a wayang play will proceed, and the exciting parts which they like to watch: the fight scenes and, in particular, the moment when the hero appears with his servants at midnight. Attending a performance creates a bond and, in view of the traditional religious significance of wayang, this is not surprising. According to tradition, everyone at a wayang performance is safe from the evil influences which normally plague people – even though they may be so far from the screen that they can barely hear the voice of the *ḍalang* (puppeteer).

Different types of wayang

A wayang is a flat or round puppet used for puppet shows on Java. *Wayang* is also the word used for plays featuring characters or stories from the wayang repertoire; human actors or three-dimensional wooden puppets can also perform in these plays. The word can also be used to mean the traditional Javanese values depicted in wayang theatre.

There are various types of wayang, but this book will focus on wayang purwå, the most important type of wayang on Java, which uses *kulit* (flat leather puppets), whose shadows are projected on a large

Left: Wayang purwå performance on the occasion of a wedding in a Javanese village, c. 1930.

white screen. *Wayang purwå* makes use of the *purwå* repertoire: the oldest stories are about the beginning of the world, the struggle between demons and gods, and the early kings. The most important stories and characters from the purwå repertoire will be described in the last section of this book.

Other forms of wayang make use of different types of puppets. *Wayang klitik* or *krucil* (*klitik* and *krucil* refer to something small or something which makes a tinkling or clattering sound) uses flat, painted wooden puppets cut in bas-relief, with leather arms. For performances, a frame which is only suggestive of a screen replaces the standard screen. In central Java this type of wayang presents tales from the Damar Wulan repertoire, stories about a grass-cutter and stable-boy who becomes the king of Majapahit after having many adventures. In eastern Java there are often performances from the Panji cycle, stories from eastern Javanese Hindu realms between the 11th and 13th century, about the adventures of a legendary hero, Prince Panji and his bride, Princess Cåndråkirånå.

Three-dimensional wooden puppets that are painted and clothed are employed in *wayang golek* (*golek*: doll). On central Java, wayang golek utilises the tales about the Arab prince, Amir Hamzah, an uncle of the prophet Mohammed; the rise of wayang golek in this area is closely linked to the popularization of Islam. On western Java, where wayang golek is much more popular than wayang kulit, the performances are derived from the purwå repertoire.

Apart from the above-mentioned wayang performances with puppets, three other forms of wayang exist: *wayang wong*, *wayang topeng*, and *wayang beber*. *Wayang wong* (*wong*: human) is acted out and danced by actors dressed as wayang puppets who also speak the dialogues. Chants and recitations are spoken by a dalang. This is somewhat different to *wayang topeng* (*topeng*: mask), in which the story is acted by actors wearing masks but the plot is narrated by a dalang. In *wayang beber* (*beber*: to show, to roll out), long lengths of textile or bark paper are used on which the sequence of painted wayang scenes is depicted.

Left: *Topeng*, mask, representing Petruk, 22 cm, c. 1900. Histrionic but magically potent Petruk, a son of Semar.
Above: *Topeng*, mask, representing princess Srikandi, 17.5 cm. Srikandi, the militant second wife of Arjunå, is a champion in archery, an art she was taught by her husband.
Page 14/15: Wayang golek performance, c. 1930.

During the recital of the story, the paintings are slowly unfurled from a pole, and rolled up again on another pole, thus showing the various scenes to the audience. This rare type of wayang is performed in remote areas of central Java during cleansing rituals. The repertoire is derived from wayang purwå or Damar Wulan.

The origins of wayang

Wayang purwå was originally found only on Java and Bali, and other places where Javanese people settled, such as southern Sumatra, south Borneo and Surinam.

Although the origins of wayang purwå have been subject to intense scholarly debate in the last part of the 19th and the beginning of the 20th centuries, its precise origins remain elusive. Wayang is clearly of Javanese origin with animistic features, but over the centuries it was influenced by many foreign cultures as a result of the many traders and immigrants who visited the island.

Originally it was not individuals who were depicted on stage but legendary beings. These mythical figures, represented by the most important puppets, were used to explain the relationship between heaven and human society, and the origin and structure of the world. The introduction of narratives, such as the Indian epics, increased the number of puppets and brought more individuality to the characters.

The oldest images in a style clearly reminiscent of wayang are the narrative reliefs on east Javanese temples dating from the 13th and 14th centuries BC. In the heyday of the east Javanese kingdoms, Javanese views on how to depict various roles acquired a fixed form. The figures are depicted as flat, in high relief, and stylized. Their dress is of the type still worn at official court ceremonies, including *dodot* (a garment of state). Perhaps the wayang puppets at that time looked like the images on the temples. In many ways the Balinese puppets can be seen as a continuation of the Javanese puppets as they had been before the advent of Islam. The north Balinese puppets in particular look more human and are more voluminous, not as spirit-like and thin as the Javanese puppets. The style of southern Bali is more like that of Java.

Around the beginning of the 1st century AD, Chinese sources mention small Hindu kingdoms on Java. Hindu civilization was imported by Brahmin priests in the wake of traders from India. Local kings took them into their service to consolidate their power, most likely because Brahmanic teachings contributed to their authority. The new concepts from India probably blended easily with local traditions and beliefs. Indian legends also made their way to Java, and the divine heroes from these stories are featured in the wayang plays. A stone inscription from central Java dating from 907 AD mentions a "wayang performance held in honour of the gods". From this inscription, and later ones, it must be concluded that if wayang performances were common around 900 AD, then they must be considerably older.

Trade with China had existed since the 1st century AD but unlike Indian influences, which affected language and world views at the royal courts, Chinese influences were limited to material aspects of Javanese culture such as the form and style of common utensils and technical skills. Chinese influence on wayang has not been very great, but it is sometimes evident in the colours and decorative motifs on wayang kulit figures in the style typical of the northern coast of Java, known as the *Pasisir* (coast) culture. This area had been an international trading centre for centuries. In the 13th century it was reached by Islamic traders. Frequent exposure to foreigners introduced the inhabitants of the coast to new ideas, which were accepted as long as they did not conflict with their own. Pasisir culture, developed from the constant adaptation of old ideas and adoption of new ones, has contributed greatly to the typical courtly culture of central Java.

Islam originated in Arabia, and by the time it reached the islands of Indonesia, it had come a long way, most often by way of traders from India. Suffused with popular, pre-Islamic mystical ideas, the new religion must have impressed the Javanese with their animist belief that

Page 18/19: Wayang beber was still rarely performed until 1900. This is a special performance for Dutch linguist G.A.J. Hazeu, in the palace of Yogyakarta, 1902.
Page 20/21: Wayang wong performance at the court of Mangku Negàrà, c. 1900. The leading parts were played by princes.

everything had a soul. This led to a new mystical interpretation of wayang performances which was incorporated into existing Javanese views on wayang. A Javanese legend says that the Wali, the holy men who brought Islam to Java, are the real creators and popularizers of wayang, which they used to teach the people to accept the new religion. There is certainly some truth in this. The spread of Islam was accompanied by a popularization of the culture that had previously been limited to the royal courts. This stands in contrast to the severe and principled form of Islam which developed later, and was not open to new ideas, even condemning and prohibiting wayang.

The principalities of central Java, with Yogyakarta and Surakarta as the main centres, have been influential in developing new wayang ideas. Various innovations were made by monarchs over the centuries. New characters were added, features or colours of the puppets were altered, and new styles were created. For example, Raden Patah from Demak expanded the number of puppets so that the stories from the Ramayana and Mahabharata could be performed; under Sunan Agung from Mataram, different eye shapes were developed for different characters; Paku Buwånå I from Kartåsurå was the first to distinguish *sabrangan*, wayang characters from outside Java, and Hamengku Buwånå I from Yogyakarta was responsible for the development of the special Yogyakartan style.

In the 19th century, the last great influx of new foreign ideas took root. These were introduced by the schools set up by the Dutch colonial government. Although there was frequent contact with Europeans in the preceding centuries, it was the Dutch who taught European methods and ways of thinking to many Javanese people.

In the 20th century, and after independence in particular, a veritable cultural revolution occurred in Java: for the first time, large numbers of Javanese left their country to study abroad for lengthy periods of time. Western ideas were rapidly incorporated into Javanese culture. With respect to wayang, this is evident in the informative and propagandizing functions that some types of wayang acquired, and in the schools where

Left: Wayang wong headdress for the role of Bimå, 20th century, central Java.

23

Right: Prince from Yogyakarta in wayang wong dress, representing Arjunå, c. 1920.

Page 26: Two klitik puppets, 36.5 and 48.5 cm, c. 1900 or earlier, east Java. To the left, the jester Sapdåpalon. This figure belongs to the Damar Wulan epos, which is thought to follow the purwå era, and originates from 15th-century east Java. Accordingly he wears a *kris* (dagger). There is a tuft of human hair on his head as a token of his importance. You can see Limbuk to the right, the dumb and permanently lovesick servant, slow of speech and wit, who is one of the public's darlings because of her dialogues with other Pånåkawan.

Page 27: Two klitik puppets, 48 and 44 cm, c. 1900 or earlier, east Java. To the left, one of the haughty and cheating cousins of Damar Wulan, Layang Setå or Layang Kumitir. To the right, Menak Jinggå with dog's head and clubfoot.

classes of future dalang (puppeteers), the directors of the wayang performance, are taught with Western-style textbooks. The first wayang conference was organized in 1969 in the Indonesian capital, Jakarta. Dalang from the most remote mountain villages were invited, and each existing type of wayang was demonstrated with a performance. It must have been a revelation to the interested viewers. Previously, most of the knowledge of people interested in wayang had been limited to their own regions. Now people could see that there were many types and styles of wayang with their own eyes. The goals of the conference included the documentation of existing types of wayang, attempting to preserve rare types of wayang, promoting wayang and, if possible, rallying government support. A special wayang museum opened in Jakarta in 1975.

Wayang tradition in everyday life

Wayang characters can greatly influence people's lives. They function as role models, and their ideals can become fashionable, thus influencing an entire generation. For example, Arjunå, the 'perfect man', and Yudistirå, the thoughtful and gentle king divorced from earthly desires, represented ideals of an older generation. With later generations, Gatotkåcå was more popular. He is the valorous hero who dies as a young man by giving his life for Arjunå. Gatotkåcå was associated with the young men who gave their lives for their country in the war for independence.

In the light of animist beliefs, the Javanese ascribe power to names, and parents like to give their children names from wayang. The name is chosen carefully because it will influence the character and life of the child. Only the passage of time will reveal whether a chosen name suits its bearer. Illnesses, accidents, and other misfortunes can indicate an inappropriate choice. Such occurrences are seen as evidence that the name is not in harmony with its bearer, so another name must be

Live broadcast of a wayang performance.
Studio Radio Republik Indonesia, 1969.

sought. President Soekarno's original name was Kusnô. Because of his poor health, his parents decided on a different name, and he was named after Karnå, the *satriå* (nobleman). In his youth, Soekarno signed his nationalist newspaper articles with the name of the warrior Bimå.

Many wayang expressions have become part of daily speech, and situations and events are talked about in analogy with wayang. An example of thinking in terms of wayang is the interpretation of events during the political changes of 1965. An analysis of the Javanese interpretations of these events suggests that everything is a reflection of classical wayang drama. The *gårå-gårå* is a passage in wayang plays where there are ominous portents in the form of natural disasters prior to the big battle: the eruption of the Merapi in eastern Java and the Agung on Bali had cost many lives and many failed harvests. The Bråtåyudå, the Great War of the Mahabharata which is seldom performed because of its dangerous negative power, except for the 'total' ritual cleansing of a village, had become reality. As in the wayang stories, two large factions, two branches of a single family, faced each other in a life and death struggle. The legendary prophecies of Jåyåbåyå, a 12th-century king of Kediri would come true, and the age of the kingdom of the *Ratu Adil* (the Just King) was near.

Wayang performances are given on the occasion of important social or domestic events to ensure good fortune or to ward off calamity. The main criterion is an important change, sometimes entering a 'higher stage' of life. This needs to be marked by the performance of the appropriate play, through which the new balance in relations is strengthened.

At a wedding, *Partå Kråmå*, the story of Arjunå's wedding, or *Suyudånå Rabi*, the wedding of Suyudånå, may be performed. *Tingkeban*, the celebration of the seventh month of a first pregnancy, and less often *Pupak puser*, the withering of the umbilical cord, are occasions for a wayang play describing the birth of a hero, such as *Jabang Tutukå* about the birth of Gatotkåcå, *Lahiripun Permadi* about the birth of Arjunå, or *Bimanyu Lahir*, about the birth of Abimanyu. For the occasion of circumcision, a Muslim event, there is no specific play. Since it is a ceremony where the child experiences some pain but also takes a step on the road to maturity, suitable plays are those which tell about a feat such as the abduction of a princess, or winning a contest in which divine intervention solves a problem and the winner often weds a princess.

Kaul, making a promise which needs to be fulfilled when a wish comes true, or unexpected luck or success, such as winning a lottery, being promoted, passing an examination, or recovering from illness, are also celebrated with a wayang performance. On such occasions plays are performed in which the Pandåwå receive a favour or a revelation from the gods. One example is the story *Arjunå Wiwåhå*, in which

Arjunå is a hermit. He is asked by the gods to help them, and his reward is the nymph Supråbå. Other examples are *Jålåtundå*, in which Durnå gives Arjunå a mighty weapon, or the story *Sumbådrå*, in which Sumbådrå dies but is resurrected.

Another occasion for a wayang performance is *bersih-deså*, the rite of cleansing the village, which is held each year after the rice harvest to commemorate the first farmer of the village. Suitable plays are *Mikukuhan*, in which the rice goddess Dewi Sri is transformed into a

crop, *Sri Måhåpunggung*, in which the goddess Dewi Sri chases away
the vermin threatening the crop, or *Sri Mantuk*, in which Dewi Sri
returns to the abode of the gods. The appropriate play for warding off
ngruwat (calamity), is *Purwåkålå*, which mentions the occasions for
which a *ngruwat* feast should be held.

All these plays are supposed to have a favourable influence. Plays
in which wars or other disasters bring enormous changes for the heroes
are believed to bring bad luck, and are only performed occasionally.

Puppets

Construction of the puppets

The puppets used in Javanese wayang purwå performances are *wayang kulit*, flat puppets made of painted leather. Buffalo leather is the preferred construction material, not only because it can be made thinner or thicker, but also because it is fairly impervious to climate changes. The leather mainly comes from *kebo wanci pengaron*, two- to three-year-old buffalos, at the best age to be hitched in front of a plough in the rice fields. This *kulit gudel* leather is fine, flexible, and easy to work with. Dry skin needs more preparation but is less fatty, so it is an ideal base for colouring.

The fresh skin is first carefully sun-dried, then soaked in a calcium solution for two or three days and nights so that it becomes supple and the hair can be removed easily. The skin is then stretched across a wooden or bamboo frame in the sun. When it has dried sufficiently it is scraped clean and smooth with a *pangot*, a short, sharp knife, until it is the desired thickness. Moistened once again, the skin is polished with a rag and put on the frame to dry for five days. The skin is then rolled and stored in a warm, well-ventilated space, a kitchen for example. The scraped buffalo skin is called *kulit sakebar*, and wayang designs will not be applied to it until eight years later.

Another frequently used, quicker way to prepare a skin is to rub it with a mixture of water and quicklime and leave it for a few days. The figures can then be cut out and given wayang charactereristics. However, the chance that the paint will peel off the leather is greater.

To make the work easier the skin is cut into two or three pieces, each called *kulit sakacu*. Traditionally, wayang figures are etched on each piece with an *untu walang*, a metal pen, but nowadays they are

Left: The wayang maker first outlines the figures according to a template. Here he is chiselling holes. Below: While playing, the children practice chiselling holes in leather.

A buffalo skin is stretched to dry on a frame in a wayang maker's house. South of Yogyakarta, 1972.

first drawn out in pencil and then traced with ink. The larger figures are drawn on thicker skin, the smaller ones on thinner skin. Next, the figures are cut out, and are then called *lakaran*.

To make it easier for the dalang to manipulate the puppets, the leather has to be thicker at the feet. The shoulders should be thin, because the arms that will be attached need to be flexible. The head should not be too thin, but thick enough to show the profile of the figure clearly. The parts to be perforated should be thinner so that the motifs stand out.

The clothing, the decorations, and the hair of the puppets are chiselled out on a wooden anvil with special chisels and a *ganden*, a small wooden hammer. At this stage, the puppets are called *gebingan*, meaning something that has been cut out, a candidate for wayang. The next important step is the creation of the face by cutting out the nose, teeth, and finally the eyes, since this will determine the puppet's character. This work is called *ambedah* (breaking open, or tilling, as with a new field for crops). For some figures the lines of facial and body hair are cut in with a fine small knife. The puppet is now ready for *nyungging* (colouring).

The basic paints used to colour puppets are *oyan* (Chinese lampblack), *gincu* (Chinese red), *atal watu* (yellow ochre), *bakaran balung* (bone-ash white), and *nilå werdi* (indigo blue). In addition, the puppets are gilded or, if that is too expensive, painted with bronze paint. Mixtures of the five basic colours yield other colours, but the puppet is covered in a white ground before colouring. To make the paints, the colours are mixed with *ancur lempeng* (carpenter's glue) and *kulit buah kepoh* (lye extracted from the skin of the *jangkang* fruit). After painting and gilding, the puppets are flattened between two thick planks covered in fabric.

Upper and lower arms and legs that have been cut out in the meantime are attached by means of a *teteg* (leather or bone pivot); the sticks for manipulating the puppets can then be attached. To enable the puppet to stand, it is clamped between two halves of a *gapit* (partially split stick), which is very fine at the figure's head and increasingly thicker towards the handle. The *gapit* is attached with coconut fibre or with red cotton thread. The preferred material for the *gapit* is horn from a *banteng* (wild buffalo) or from the albino ox from Sulawesi. For figures with a black body, black horn from the common Indonesian water buffalo is used. This horn is cheaper and easier to acquire than that of a *banteng*, so it is often used, as is bamboo, which is even cheaper.

The horns need to be 60 cm to 70 cm long, and are first split lengthwise. Sections are then sawn out, and sawn open to give it the form of a *gapit*. Both the handle and the tip which will run up to the puppet's headgear come from the top of the horn. The middle part, that is to be attached at the puppet's hips, is from the base of the horn. The *guba-han* (middle section) is the weakest part. The *gapit* is heated here, and bent until the original curvature has almost totally disappeared.

The *cempurit* (sticks for the arms) are made from the same material as the *gapit*. The length of the *cempurit* needs to be the same as the shoulder height of the puppet. The *cempurit* is fastened to the hands with coconut fibre, cotton thread or pivots.

Right: Cross section of an ox horn, with an enclosed *gapit*. The *gapit* and *cempurit* for four puppets can be made from one horn.

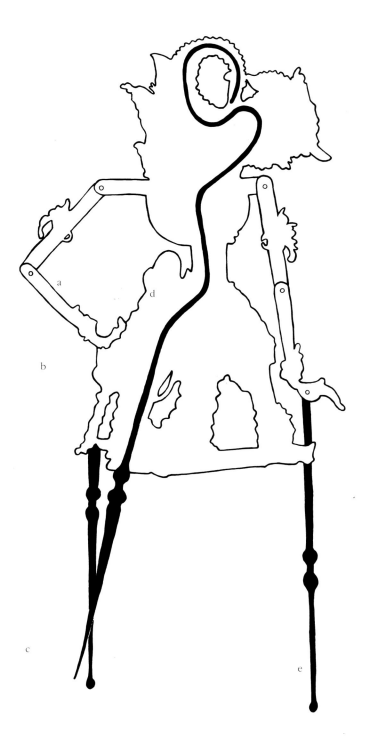

The outline of a wayang figure, in which the course of the *gapit* is indicated.

a. *gegel* (joint): the place where the upper and lower arm are connected.

b. *teteg*: bone or leather hinge which is used to connect the movable parts.

c. *cempurit*: arm rod.

d. *gubahan*: the part of the *gapit* where the section of the horn was bent.

e. *antup* (barb, point): the end of the *gapit*, with which the puppet is stuck into a banana tree trunk during a performance.

Iconography

In the 17th century, the number of wayang puppets used at the (by then Islamic) royal courts of central Java had grown, and their form became increasingly refined. Various versions of the same character in more than one guise – different ages, disguises and moods – augmented their numbers even more. For example, Arjunå appears as a youth (Janåkå, Permadi), adult (Arjunå), and hermit (Mintåtågå). Another example is Kresnå who, as a youth, is not yet wearing a crown, his hair is half long and his face points upward. Things become even more complicated when one character is represented by various puppets, each representing a mood *(wåndå)*. Particular *wåndå* are wrathful, powerful, sorrowful, peaceful, etc. However, each puppet is recognized by the audience, because each character has its own characteristics.

It is important to note that all figures and props belong to fixed categories. The *katongan* represent the kings and queens, princes and princesses; *putran* represent the nobles; *putren* include the noble ladies; *pårå dewå* include the gods; *panditå* include the wise men, hermits and teachers; *patih punggåwå* include grandees and lower court officials; *pårå danåwå* include giants, giantesses and demonic beings; *pårå wanårå* include the monkeys; *dagelan* include *pånåkawan* (male and female servants); *ricikan* include armies, vehicles, animals, letters, jars, fruit, etc.; *dadamel warni-warni* include various types of weapons.

The personality of the characters can be deduced from stature, stance, shape of the eyes, and face and body colour. Social position is indicated by clothing and ornaments. The Javanese classify the puppets into *alus* (distinguished), and *kasar* (coarse).

o

Stature

A large stature symbolizes great physical strength, a violent nature or a lack of self-control. This is in contrast to well-proportioned medium size figures, which do possess self-control and finesse. Sizes vary from 23 cm to more than 100 cm.

A slim, small body is the indication of refinement. The bodies of moderate characters are medium sized (*pidekså*), bodies of coarse characters are largest and most heavy *(ageng inggil)*.

Face

Personality is portrayed with the face, especially through the shape of the eyes and the nose. There is great variation in eyes, noses, mouths and shapes of bodies occurring in all sorts of combinations which result in detailed individual expressions. There are at least thirteen different shapes of eyes and noses. For example, the most noble characters have elongated, slanted eyes, appearing half closed (*liyepan*, or *jaitan*, 'sewn together', or *gabahan*, 'like a grain of rice'), and a *lincip* (long pointed) nose. The mouth is half closed, and the teeth are visible.

The 'intermediary' type has eyes shaped like *kedelen* (soya beans), rounder than *liyepan*, but still elongated. The nose is long and 'well-shaped' *(sembådå)* and slightly turned up at the end. The coarse, physically powerful or violent type has round wide-open eyes (*telengan*, or with a round pupil). The base of the nose is strongly accentuated, and the nose is bulbous. The mouth is open in a grin, with the fat lips revealing two rows of teeth, including incisors.

a

b

c

d

Above: The four most important eye shapes, each indicating specific characteristics:
a. *liyepan* (half-shut), *gabahan* (like a grain of rice), *jaitan* (sewn together). Belong to the most noble, very refined characters.
b. *kedelen* (like a soya bean). Belong to the intermediary type.
c. *telengan* (with round pupil). Belong to physically strong, or emotional types.
d. *pananggalan* (like the new moon). There are only a few characters who have this eye shape, among them the priest Durnå, and Batårå Narådå, the messenger of the gods.
Page 40, left: Hermit-king Abiåså, 48 cm, 19th century, Cirebon, west Java. King Abiåså, grandfather of the Pandåwå and Koråwå, with a *garudå mungkur*, a royal piece of jewellery, and a *garudå* head as a sign of his royal status.
Page 40, right: Kresñå, 54 cm, 19th century, Cirebon, west Java.

Posture

The positions of the head and feet are also indications of character. A *tumungkul* (bowed head) means that the hero is *sabar* (patient), *mungkul* (dedicated) and *sareh* (calm), three characteristics which are among the highest virtues. A head held high *(langak)* means the opposite: impatience, aggression and irritability. Facing straight ahead *(longok)* is 'neutral' and does not indicate any special characteristic.

The position of the feet varies from close together, indicating circumspection, to wide apart, expressing speed and capability.

Colour

Face and body colour also indicate a figure's character. Originally, the four main colours (black, red, gold and white) were connected to the classification system of early Javanese thought. This classification draws on the inter-relationship between groups of things which, to the non-Javanese, seem to be totally unconnected, such as colours, units of the calendar, parts of the heavens, numbers, animals, plants, emotions, etc. For mental states, black denoted imbalance and rigidity; red denoted covetousness and a desire to control everything; yellow denoted a desire to flaunt and vanity; and white denoted a capacity to absorb everything. Multiple colours denoted eloquence.

The existence of such colour classifications indicates a conviction that there is unity and equilibrium in everything that exists. The ancient cosmological meaning has been mostly lost, and today the colours have different meanings, more related to the individual's character. Black indicates maturity and tranquillity; red signifies uncontrolled passion and desire; white is used somewhat arbitrarily, and can indicate noble lineage, youth or beauty; yellow indicates beauty or royal dignity. Puppet makers may also use gold to embellish the puppet. Younger figures generally have lighter colours than older ones. Some important figures have a lighter or more golden body colour before midnight than after. Today, colours other than the traditional base colours are also used. Shades of pink and purple are used for red, blue is used for black, and brown and grey are used for some animals and giants.

Noble figures have black, gold or white faces and black or gold bodies. The faces of intermediary characters are black, blue, pink or red, and their bodies are coloured gold. The larger figures have pink or red faces, and their bodies are painted gold or a pale shade of pink.

Dress: clothing, headdress and jewellery

The puppet's dress indicates social status and function. Most characters are dressed in a *kain*, the typical Javanese loincloth, which can be worn in different ways. Some characters are dressed in *dodot*, the royal dress. This cloth is larger than the common *kain*, and is draped intricately. The *dodot* is worn with long silk trousers made of *cinde* fabric, with its checkered pattern. Female characters are dressed in a *kain* reaching the ankles, sometimes in combination with a *dodot*.

Further distinctions are the different types of headdress: crowns in various shapes are worn by characters of royal descent; turbans are worn by hermits, priests and holy teachers; and headcloths are worn by officials. The hair is always black, worn either loose or dressed in a knot.

The jewellery of characters belonging to the nobility is usually standardised: bracelets for the lower and upper arm, necklaces, anklets, rings. Almost every character wears a *sumping*, a piece of jewellery which is worn behind the ear. A sash indicating a caste however, is only worn by members of the *satriå* (nobility) and *wesiå* (court officials). The *badong*, a jewelled breastplate in the shape of a half moon, with three or four pendants, is only worn in combination with a state robe.

Above: *Bokongan raton*, the royal manner of
draping the loincloth, and a *kalung ulur ulur*,
a long necklace with a snake's head at the end,
indicating the caste of the person wearing it.
Centre: *Bokongan rapekan*.
Below: *Katongan* and a *kalung ulur ulur*.

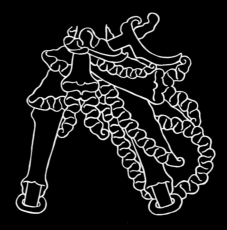

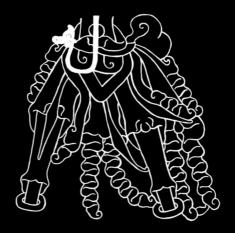

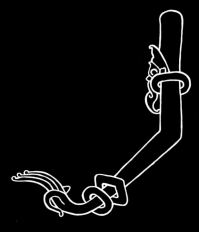

From top to bottom: Arm, hand and bracelets of the refined type, of a demon king, and of Bìmà with the typical *pàncànàkà* (sharp thumbnail).

Above: *Supit urang* ('like a lobster claw') hairstyle.
Centre: *Ketu udeng*, headdress for a court official,
such as *patih*
Below: *Ketu dewa*, headdress for a god.

Above: *Ketu pandita*, headdress for a priest.
Centre: *Makuta* (crown), *jamang* (diadem), and *garuda mungkur*.
Below: *Jamang* and *garuda mungkur*.

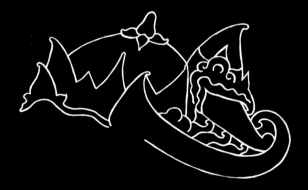

47

Animals and props

The animals in the wayang plays include monkeys, the *garuḍå* (mythological sun bird), and the *någå* (mythological snake). The monkeys are easily recognized by their long curling tail, small nose, and wide-open mouth with sharp teeth and incisors. They are dressed like humans and can speak. The *garuḍå* has a crown, and a beak with sharp teeth and two fangs. It is depicted with spread wings. The *någå* is a snake with a short curling body, whose erect crowned head displays sharp teeth and a split tongue. Like the *garuḍå*, the *någå* is able to speak.

The *perampogan* and *gunungan* or *kayon* are the most important props. The *perampogan* is a large rectangle depicting an army, with the soldiers ranked in a straight line and all their lances pointing up or forwards. They are often accompanied by a cannon.

The *gunungan* (*gunung*: mountain) or *kayon* (forest) is a large figure in the shape of a leaf, on which a tree is depicted with several animals and birds. Sometimes there is a gate flanked by two demon guards. This prop is used to signal the beginning and the end of the performance, strong emotions, scene changes, and the elements of fire, earth, air and water. It is the backdrop with which time and space are delineated, and it determines the atmosphere.

Left: Bird, 24 cm, c. 1900, Kraton Kasepuhan, Cirebon, west Java. This bird is possibly a god or demon whose appearance has been changed by a spell or a temporary disguise.

Page 50: Ki Satip, Semar's penis, 40.5 x 17 cm,
c. 1900 or earlier, Kraton Kasepuhan, Cirebon,
west Java. The penis is used by its owner as an
infallible weapon in war. In this case it has the
shape of the head of a young bull, and is made
with a fragment of an old wayang, a demon's head.
Left: *Kris*, 17.5 cm, 19th century, Cirebon, west
Java. A prop often used in fights between two
champions, for example between Arjuna and
his traditional opponent, Cakil, the ogre.

Page 52: Old Nāga and Baṭara Guru, 73 and 51 cm, 19th century, Kraton Kasepuhan, Cirebon, west Java. The old Nāga (left) is dressed as a hermit. The Nāga is associated with water, from which the first forms of life originate.

Left: Celestial tiger, 40 cm, late 19th or early 20th century, east Java. As the wayang repertoire was usually transmitted orally, many of the stories have unfortunately been lost or have not yet been recorded. It is also conceivable that some puppets have never been used for performance, but were made solely as an expression of literary and poetic creativity. It is not yet known in which story this celestial tiger featured.

Page 54: *Macam*, mythical tiger, 60 cm, c. 1900, Kraton Kasepuhan, Cirebon, west Java.

Page 55: *Kapal*, horse as a mount for a prince, 60.5 cm, end 19th century, Cirebon, west Java. On Java, five colour categories are applied to horses: black, brown, yellow, white, and piebald. Each colour is further defined by different shades. Dark brown is considered the most beautiful colour. All kinds of other characteristics are important as well, for example, the directions of the growth of the horse's hair, because they are believed to say something about the characteristics of the horse, and are also supposed to tell the future for the horse's owner.

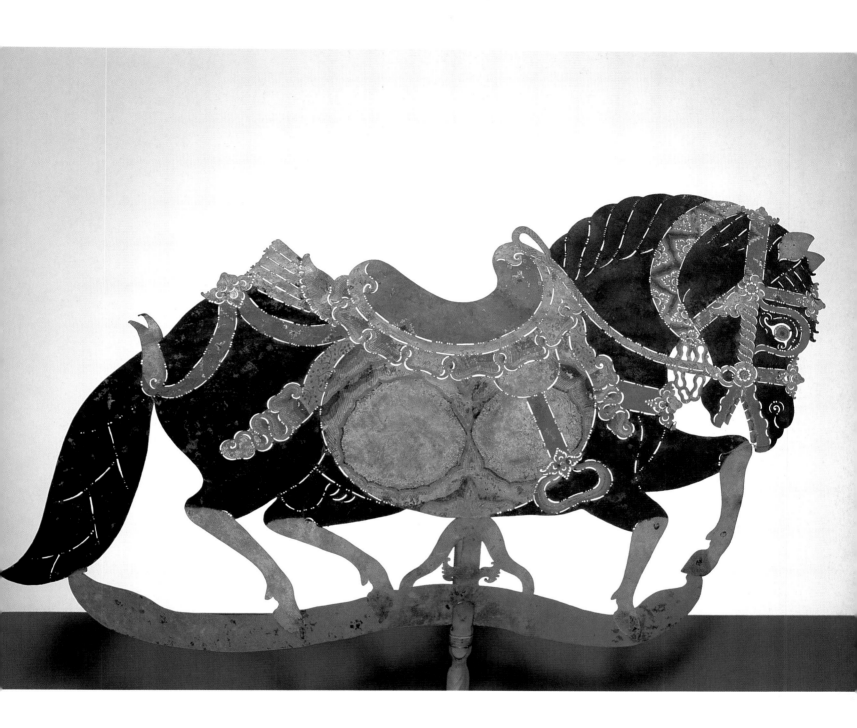

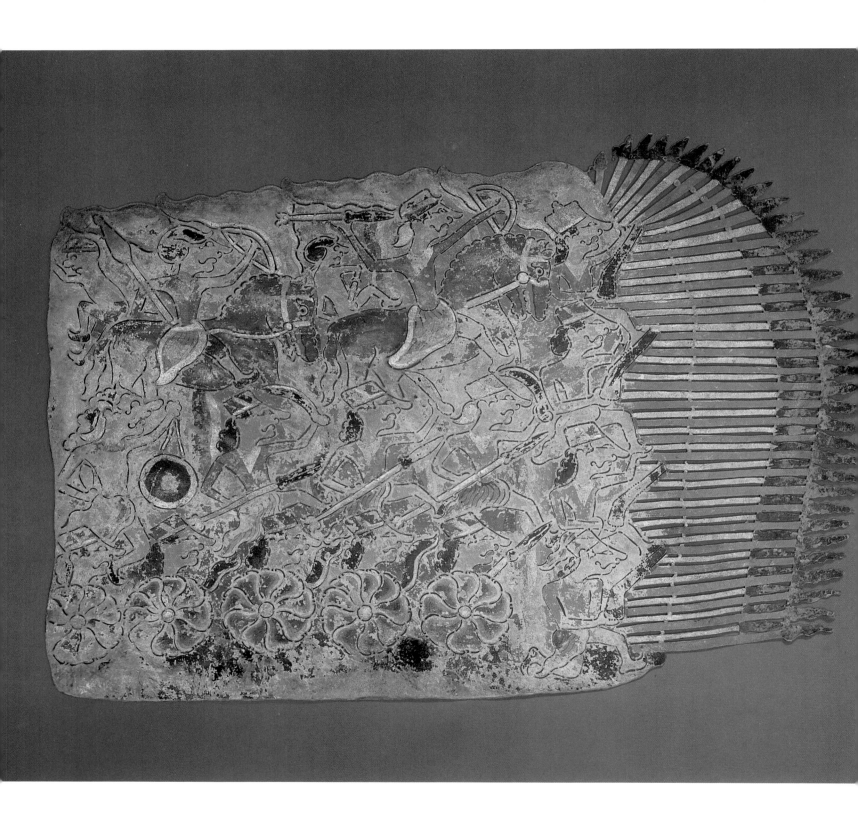

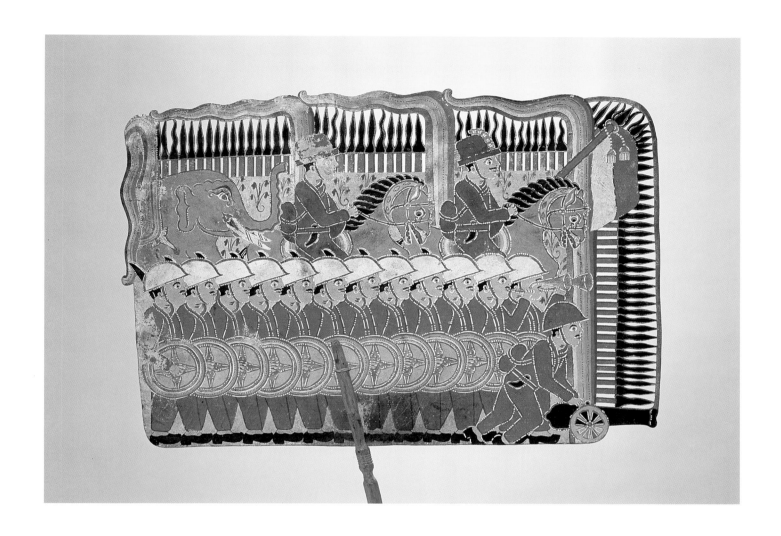

Left: *Perampogan*, army, 43 cm, c. 1850 or later, Kraton Kasepuhan, Cirebon, west Java. An army from the 'good' side is well-organized and only has human soldiers, whereas an army from the 'bad' side has demon soldiers as well as human ones. This *perampogan* is clearly of a more disorderly nature: humans take to the battlefield alongside demons, and they all swing along together in a belligerent manner, with old-fashioned arms such as spears, blunderbusses, daggers, lances, and shields. Above: *Perampogan*, army, 42 cm, after 1960, Principalities, central Java.

Right: A typical modern *gunungan*, 86 cm, c. 1960, Surakarta, central Java. According to Bosch, the most important requisite in wayang theatre, the *gunungan* (mountain) or *kayon* (forest), is a representation of the ancient Tree motif originating from India. This consists of two parts, a mountain and a tree.

The Tree motif is rendered as a combination of two different trees, the fig tree rooted in heaven, and the (earthbound) lotus tree rising from the waters. The former, placed above, has implanted its root in the top of the stem of the tree-shaped lotus. The lotus is the very symbol of life springing from the waters. The celestial fig tree represents 'creative breath' or fire, which is as essential in creating life as the water's essence. In the Javanese *gunungan*, the lotus part can assume an hourglass form, with a small building with a pair of closed doors, or that of a lake or pot filled with water. Guardians stand on both sides of the stronghold. Their task is to guard treasures, particularly the Meru (heavenly mountain), and the liquid elixir of life. A pair of huge wings flank the upper half. These wing shapes may actually be derived from lotus leaves or other vegetation.

The tall gate building with closed doors can be understood as female, whereas the tree represents the male. Together and united they form life. The *banteng* (wild buffalo) here symbolizes earth, matter and fertility. The tiger represents fire, sky and spirit.

Page 59: *Gunungan*, 74.5 cm, late 19th or early 20th century, Kraton Kasepuhan, Cirebon, Pasisir, west Java. A grotto-like mound rises from what seems to be a blackish pool of water, flanked by two lotus flowers on long stems. There is a monster's head sitting on it, like those crowning the gates of the 8th-century Buddhist temple, Borobudur, a head with no lower jaw. This head is highly stylized, a characteristic of Islam-influenced Hindu-Buddhist art on Java, of which Cirebon is in many ways the epitome.

Page 60/61: *Gunungan blumbangan*, 67.5 cm, 19th century, Pasisir, north coast of Java. One side of this *gunungan* is an abstract representation of the elements: earth, water, fire and air. The other side shows sleek, stylized animals around a lotus, with a Javanese text in its heart, characterizing it as a vehicle of *kejawen* (Javanese mysticism). *Kejawen* is of a syncretic nature, and contains traits of animism, ancestor worship, Hinduism, Buddhism and Islam. The essence of *kejawen* lies in overcoming self-interest and self-importance, its purpose is the individual's harmonious relationship with God, irrespective of worldly consequences. To this end one has to faithfully perform one's duty in the position on earth where one has been placed according to the law of karma, the law of God and the law of men. In this way one will achieve unity with the cosmic purpose. The indistinct text suggests the following syllables: *s a ka ba da r a ya*. This can be interpreted as: *sakabeh darayat àdà*, meaning: each has his own talents. These symbols remind people of their place and task in life during the wayang performance. The lotus flower holding the text is encircled by a rainbow. Around the foliage of the *kayon*, which has a basin filled with water as its base, a halo is represented in the style of those from statues of the Borobudur.

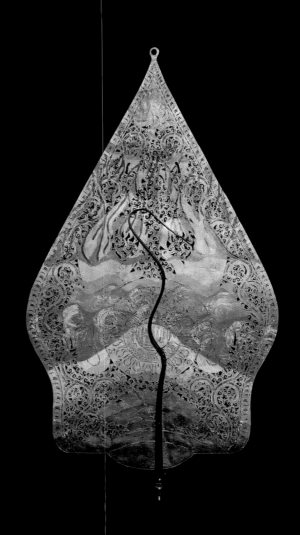

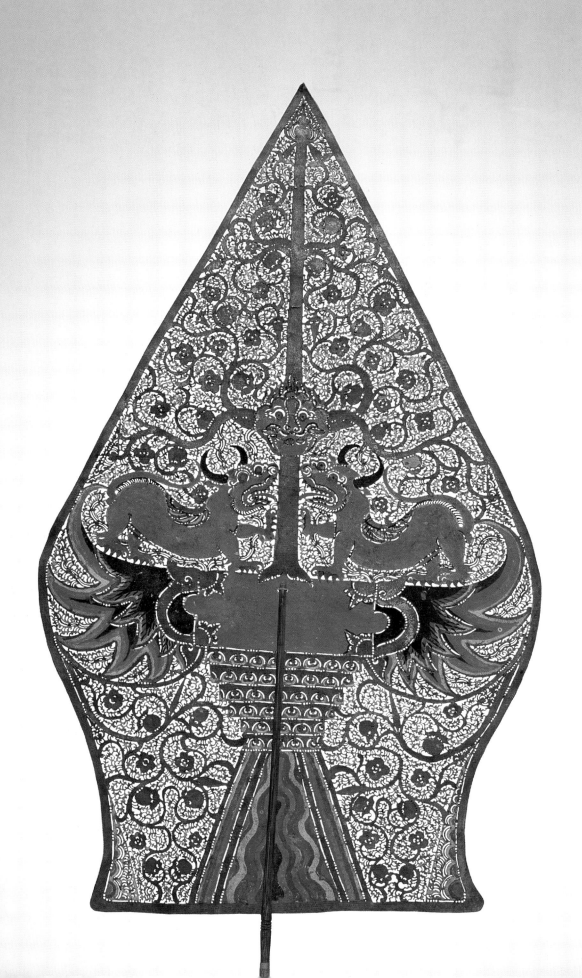

Page 62: *Kayon*, shaped as a mountain of flames, 69.5 cm, c. 1850, Kraton Kasepuhan, Cirebon, west Java. While the dalang often uses the *gunungan* to suggest a mountain, a palace, a forest, or the sea, he also uses it to represent natural phenomenona such as a storm or a blazing fire, or even as a metaphor for the devastating powers of war. This *gunungan* may have served such purposes.

Page 63: *Gunungan blumbangan*, 64 cm, 19th century, Pasisir, north coast of Java. Two horned animals with long tails scratch the trunk of the Tree of Heaven. Just above their heads is a monster's head, situated precisely where the Tree of Heaven, the ficus, is attached to the Tree of the Waters, the lotus. Here, the tree rises from a small lake resting on an hourglass-shaped elevation. The elegant ramification of the tree branches undulates all the way down to the ground, almost encircling the base of the mountain symbol.

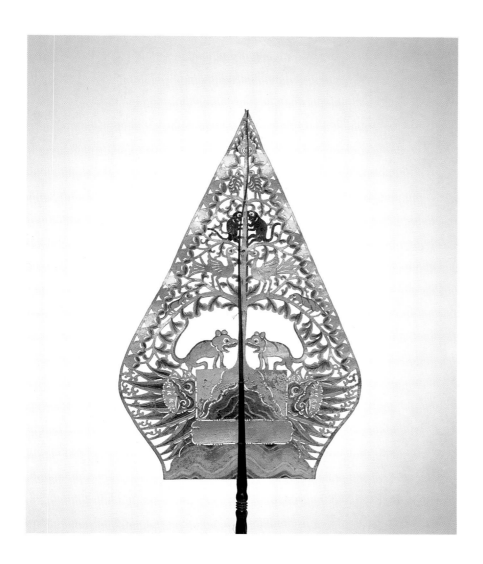

Page 64: *Gunungan blumbangan* (*blumbangan*: pond), 64.5 cm, 19th century, Pasisir, north coast of Java. Two horned animals with long tails scratch the trunk of the Tree of Heaven. Just above their heads is a monster's head. It is situated precisely where, according to Bosch, the Tree of Heaven, or ficus, is attached to the Tree of Waters, or lotus.

Left: *Gunungan blumbangan*, 43 cm, 19th century, Pasisir, north coast of Java. Many *gunungan* show leaves and branches densely populated with birds and other animals: the Tree of Heaven is also the Tree of Life which nourishes and sustains all creatures. Exceptionally, two feline animals are shown. Here they appear as hares or rabbits, sometimes they resemble cats or have a human form, but they are nearly always characterized by long, tapering ears. Bosch argues that they represent the twin-gods, Aswins, who are closely associated with the sun-god. They are guardians of the elixir of life, and therefore act as physicians of the gods, as donors of youth, wealth, and offspring, and as helpers of the needy. Instead of the customary monster's head halfway up the tree stem, here we see a pair of birds and a pair of monkeys.

Different styles: Yogyakarta, Surakarta and Pasisir

There are many regional differences in the styles of wayang puppets that have evolved in the course of history, including differences between the traditional cultural rivals, Surakarta and Yogyakarta. Although these differences are often negligible because of their mutual influence, each style is easily recognizable.

In general, Surakarta pays more attention to *alus* (refinement), while Yogyakarta focuses more on the *gagah* (power). In Surakarta, the wings or haloes of some figures have wavy edges, while in Yogyakarta the wing edges are smooth. Surakarta puppets have shorter arms, and the fingers are less bent, whereas Yogyakarta puppets have straight arms that reach the ground. The *kain* (loincloth) of a noble lady in Yogyakarta has folds that fall over the feet to the front; for a lady in Surakarta the fold falls behind the legs. The style of the central Javanese principalities is more or less the official standard, as can be seen from books about wayang that have appeared in Indonesia in recent decades.

The Pasisir style is the name of the style from the north coast, of which Cirebon is the most important cultural centre. The population of Cirebon has been influenced by a rich stream of spiritual ideas for centuries. As a port, Cirebon functioned as a melting pot of religious and artistic ideas, including animism with its ancestor worship, Hinduism, Buddhism and Islam. This resulted in a characteristic style in which mystic rapture brings the puppets to life, a style completely different from those of the central Javanese principalities, in which meditation and the discipline of immobility is evident. Although the style is wholly Javanese (though surprisingly close to Balinese wayang) there are differences in detail. Puppets of this style often appear old-fashioned, and seem to represent an earlier phase of central Javanese wayang. Examples of this include the Chinese-inspired, broad collars that are no longer to be seen in central Java, the different colours, and the more baroque clothing. Furthermore, various wayang figures are still used in Cirebon which no longer exist in central Java but are only mentioned by the dalang in the narrative text. The Pasisir *gunungan* and *pånåkawan* are also very different from the standard types of central Java. The figures are also more lively, though less detailed, less elaborately decorated, and less stylized. Instead of golden body colours, pastel colours such as beige, mauve, and grey are used.

The Pånåkawan

On the Javanese stage, the most pathetic scenes are often interrupted by the jokes of the *pånåkawan*, the servants of the hero. In the epics proper there is no mention of the *pånåkawan*, but they are especially important characters in the plays, and the dalangs use them to refer to contemporary issues. In wayang purwå performances this occurs especially during the *gårå-gårå*, the climax and turning-point of the performance. It is the *pånåkawan* who break the tension with their antics. There is a fine line between the sublime and the ridiculous; wisdom easily becomes foolishness and vice versa. But jokes during lofty scenes are also part of the Javanese feeling for relativity; everything is controlled by balanced, harmonious relationships. Humour and satire have a protective and strengthening power and are the counterbalance for passion, despair, and other deep feelings which may disturb the harmony with their intensity. The Javanese word for clown, *badut*, is derived from *badot*, meaning healer. Both groups are thought to be inspired by higher powers. For example, on visits to certain holy places on Java, tradition requires telling jokes, especially erotic and obscene ones, during the journey.

The *pånåkawan* are thought to be purely Javanese by origin because of their roles as mediators. In southern India there are also shadow plays around themes from the Ramayana with comical commentators: two 'ugly and grotesque Brahmin priests'.

Semar

Semar, the oldest and most important of the *pånåkawan*, was originally a god, 'the twin brother of heaven'. He is the guide of the hero on a journey full of tribulations which the hero must overcome before achieving his goal. According to the legends he is a brother of the highest god, Batårå Guru. As punishment for a misdeed he was given a grotesque form and sent to earth to serve the descendants of the gods.

Left: Sarahita, Togog, Semar, Petruk and Nålågareng, c. 1960, Surakarta, central Java. Semar's sons Sårahitå, Togog, Petruk and Nålågareng have been brought to life by Semar's practice of meditation. Behind Semar are the rheumatic Nålågareng with the club foot, and his tall younger brother, Petruk, with his big nose. To the left are Sårahitå and Togog, faithful but often unjustly treated servants of the left faction. Although serving enemy parties, the servants treat each other in a friendly way, and often the servants of the left party complain to the servants of the right party about their masters.

Semar is the most popular figure in the whole wayang repertoire. As soon as he appears, a wave of sympathy and deep respect goes through the audience. He cries easily, farts continually, is hugely fat, and has an enormous behind. However, he is a fount of wisdom, and even though he is a servant he acts as an equal, or even superior to his master.

Semar's appearance befits his nature and his place in the ancient mythological world: he is both man and woman. The creation of later *pånåkawan* was more inspired by realism and parody. The deformities and infirmities afflicting all these servants may be related to the respect or even fear that such deformed people aroused, because they were thought to consort with the spirits. At the courts, dwarfs, albinos and deformed people served as jesters, with their fixed places in processions. This practice continued until just before the Second World War.

Central Java has a different, 'western' style of wayang purwå performances to eastern Java, which has its 'eastern' style. The difference lies mainly in the groups of *pånåkawan* in the performances. The famous dalang Anjangmas (or Panjangmas), the founder of many of the traditions of professional dalangs in the Javanese principalities, lived in the second half of the 17th century. He and his wife were employed by the king of Mataram and, after the plundering of the court by the Madurese in 1677, they lived as vagabonds. *Nyai* (lady) Anjangmas was also a dalang, and is hailed as the founder of the eastern style, in which Semar performs along with Bagong and Cemuris. In the western style, introduced by her husband, Semar is accompanied by Nålågareng and Petruk. On the north coast, styles have become mixed: Semar's entourage consists of Nålågareng and Petruk as well as Bagong. The geographical border between western and eastern styles has moved eastward as the western style gained in popularity.

The following lines are the words with which the dalang introduces Semar and his sons in this 'western' style (see p. 72). The text illustrates the significance which the Javanese attach to names, which are believed to be connected to character and the way of life:

Why is he called Semar? He is called Semar for this reason: Semar comes from the word *samar* (vague). And yes, the person of the *kyai lurah* (master of secret theology) Semar can be called mysterious. Call him a man, and his face will look like a woman's; call him a woman and he will look like a man. What does *kyai lurah* Semar look like? He has a snub nose which is *mråkåteni* (so charming that it inspires love), watery eyes, puffy cheeks, also comely; he is fat, but graceful; in short, everything about his person is pleasing. Anyone in Semar's company therefore wins the love of the gods. Indeed, *kyai lurah* Semar is a mysterious person, for he is not an ordinary human but a divinity from the *Surålåyå* (heaven), in fact *Sang Hyang* (the venerable god) Ismåyå. Kyai lurah has two sons: the eldest is called *kyai lurah* Nålå-Gareng, the youngest *kyai* Petruk. Why is his name Nålå-Gareng? *Nålå* is 'heart', *gareng* means 'dry'. Nålå-Gareng has a dry heart, which is why he is always sad. What does he look like? His eyes are crossed, his lips do not close all the way, his arms are *ceko* (crooked because of a break); he is a cripple and limps, because his feet are covered in *bubul* (wounds caused by the Yaws illness). And *kyai* Petruk? His body is long, his nose is long, his eyes are long and narrow, his lips stick out, his neck is long, his legs are long, his steps are long, and his hands are long too. What is he like? He is rowdy but it makes him earn a legacy. If he steals, he is praised, if he quarrels he is praised, if he gets into a fight he is rewarded.

Left: Semar and Sekar Pandan, 43 and 34 cm, c. 1850, Kraton Kasepuhan, Cirebon, west Java. The amiable Semar with his black body and his white powdered face is wearing golden earrings. Semar is wearing a red-white *poleng* (chequered) loincloth to cover his ample hips and to support his umbilical hernia. His relative, Sekar Pandan, who is only known in the Cirebon Region, owes his long neck to a fall from heaven to earth, when he became stuck in a tree. He is dressed like Semar, but his loincloth is without the chequered pattern that averts evil.

Page 74/75: Three examples of Nålågareng, 39, 36 and 46.5 cm, all 20th century. Yogyakarta, Surakarta and Surakarta, central Java. Nålågareng is shown in his usual attire, as a woman, and as King Pandubregålå. *Pånåkawan* Nålågareng plays different roles in different plays.

Performance

Requisites

In a wayang kulit performance the shadows of the puppets are cast on to a white fabric screen *(kelir)* in a wooden frame. Over the head of the dalang, there is a special brass oil lamp *(blencong)* which is often shaped like the mythical sun bird *garuda* or like a *gunungan*. These days an electric lamp is used which gives a constant bright light, in contrast to the more lively but weaker light of the traditional oil lamp.

In front of the dalang, and parallel to the screen, there are two banana tree trunks, one a little higher than the other, into which the puppets are jabbed with their pointed handles when they are not in use. Members of the just party are placed on the right side, and members of the unjust party on the left. The highest ranking figures are placed on the higher trunk.

To the left of the dalang there is a *kotak* (rectangular chest) in which the puppets and other props are kept. The chest has some small wooden or metal plates attached to it, called *keprak* or *kecrek*, which the dalang, sitting cross-legged in front of the screen during the performance, tinkles with his right foot to indicate the fury of the elements, the din of battle or the roaring of a giant. Using his left hand, he taps the inside of the chest with a *cempålå* (small horn) or *tabuh keprak* (wooden hammer*)* to guide the *gamelan* players sitting behind him. The lid of the chest sits to the right of the dalang and contains the puppets he wants to keep handy. Near the dalang there is also a *padupan* (bowl of incense) which is lit at the beginning of the performance, and a *sajen* (bowl with sacrifices for the spirits), which might include food or flowers.

Musical accompaniment dates from as late as the eighteenth century; *gamelan* music is essential to a wayang performance, and the music is

Left: *Blencong*, wayang lamp, 81 x 51 cm, 20th century, east Java. This *blencong* is bird-like, but has a human head and body. It represents a concept derived from Hindu mythology, where it is called *kinara*.

specially selected for each performance. There are several tonal scales or modes, but in wayang purwå, the music is mostly in *salendro*, the five-tone scale of Javanese *gamelan* music, with approximately equal intervals between the tones *(barang, gulu, ḍåḍå, lima, nem)*. The music expresses the atmosphere of the various sections of the performance and accentuates the movements and words of the puppets. Some wayang characters have their own particular melodies, associated with their personalities and moods.

Page 78: *Kotak*, chest for storing wayang, 129.5 x 90 x 87 cm, c. 1880, Yogyakarta, central Java. Five scenes are carved in bas-relief on the outside of the chest, and a sixth scene inside the lid. According to the Yogyakarta style, which has retained most characteristics, old demons and monkeys are rendered with two eyes, instead of with only one as in the later Surakarta style.

Left above: *Blencong*, wayang lamp, 51 cm, 19th century, Java. This wayang lamp has the form of a *garuḍā*, with a tall royal crown on its head. It has long pendants on either side of the head. The crown is shaped like a mountain with many peaks, like the ideal Mahameru, with one distinctive peak on top, the symbol of the highest god or the utmost contemplative concentration. The rump of the bird serves as the receptacle for the oil. The outstretched wings and the spread tail feathers are meant to reflect the light when the lamp is being used.

Left below: *Blencong*, wayang lamp, in the shape of a crowned *garuḍā*, 44.5 cm, 19th century, east Java. Its iconographic characteristics are similar to those of the *blencong* above.

Page 80/81: *Sajen*, offerings for a wayang performance at the court of Surakarta, 1966.

Lakon

A *lakon*, the Javanese word for 'play', is an adaptation of the classical wayang literature for wayang performances. There are three main types of *lakon*. *Lakon pokok* (*pokok* meaning nucleus) does not deviate from official tradition, while *lakon carangan* (*carang* meaning side-branch) is derived from traditional topics. If the traditional story can be clearly recognized it is called *lakon carang kadapur* (*dapur* meaning combination). If the *lakon* has little more in common with the original story than the names of a few protagonists it is called *lakon sempalan* (*sempalan* meaning broken off or loose).

These plays are written down in *pakem* (handbooks), which contain brief outlines of the stories, with sufficient directions for their performance. Although more detailed *pakem* exist, to a large extent the performance and the recital reflect the style of the dalang, who improvises on a theme. The dalang can also base his stories on poetry or prose, but these need to be adapted to the fixed requirements of a performance.

A *lakon* is divided into fixed sections. This sequence is one of the oldest characteristics of a *lakon*, and is related to religious overtones of consecration and entering a new state. The word *lakon* is derived from *laku*, which means 'go' or 'act', but can also imply 'adventure' or 'journey'. Each section can be seen as a stop along the journey. The transition from one section to the next is marked by *suluk*, the dalang's recitative announcement of what is about to happen.

Stages of the performance

Traditionally a performance starts soon after sunset, at about 7.30 p.m., and continues without a break until dawn, at about 6.00 a.m. In the past there was a tendency to separate the audience according to gender: women sat facing the screen onto which the shadows were projected, and men sat on the other side with the dalang, where they could see

Page 82/83: Wayang performance at the court in Yogyakarta, c. 1930.

the actual puppets. The origins of this practice are religious as well as traditional, but now it is rarely encountered, especially in modern wayang, where the shadow aspect of the puppets has become less important as a result of the secularization of wayang.

At a private wayang purwå performance, the host and his guests often view the puppets from inside the house, i.e. facing the screen. But each performance attracts many people, and anyone who is interested can watch. These occasional guests, usually including many women and children, either sit with the dalang or watch from the yard.

The evening begins with an overture of *gamelan* music *(talu)* which sets the mood of the *lakon*. At a court performance this musical introduction is omitted. The dalang begins his story with the traditional eulogy to the prosperity of the kingdom and the king, let us call him King A, who then appears on stage.

When King A appears, his admirable qualities are summed up. He discusses a worrisome problem with one or more confidants (such as councillors, or sons). This indicates the theme, e.g. a daughter who is to be married, an enemy's attack, a daughter who has disappeared, or a lost son. The scene then moves to the court of King B, an enemy who is usually a non-Javanese giant 'from the other side' *(sabrangan)*. This new scene is more or less the same as the previous one. King B has plans to attack King A, or wants to marry King A's daughter, or desires a princess that King A has chosen for his own son. King A is always the righteous party on the right of the stage, and King B is on the left, representing evil. In the ensuing forest scene, the armies of King A and King B confront each other, and a first battle is fought. There is no clear victor in this *perang gagal* (undecided battle), there are no casualties, and afterwards everyone goes on their way.

It is now midnight, the magically treacherous hour when one day moves into another. The time has come for the real hero to make his appearance, and this signals the transition in the play. The hero, often in a state of inner turmoil, makes his appearance with his loyal *pånåkawan* (servants). His unrest is mirrored by *gårå-gårå* (unusual occurrences in nature), which are discussed by the servants in the form of *banyolan*, joking and tomfoolery which is meant to relieve the tension. This company then meets a group of King B's party, and a fierce fight ensues, known as the *perang kembang*. This is one of the climaxes of the performance.

The fight lasts quite a long time, and is interlarded with comical remarks and dialogues from the *pånåkawan*. Here the dalang displays all his technical expertise and eloquence, contrasting the calm and confident hero with the brute power and savage attacks of his opponent. By the end of the battle (almost 3 a.m.) the hero has prevailed. In the earlier parts of the performance, all the main characters were introduced and the theme clearly defined. By this point, all the ingredients for an exciting story with a happy ending have been brought together. The rest of the *lakon* develops this further, and there is a general battle between the two parties, called *perang tanggung* (*tanggung* meaning 'not yet finished'). In the final battle (*perang sampak, sampak* meaning 'resolution, return of equilibrium'), victory is attained by the righteous party. The performance ends with a *slametan* (collective ritual feast) for the victorious party, or a wedding.

Status and skills of the dalang

A dalang is highly respected, and is often believed to possess supernatural qualities (especially healing) because of his position as mediator between people, gods and spirits. Linguistically, the word *dalang* is thought to be associated with *langlang*, which means 'to go round' something. A dalang is a 'wanderer', but also a 'diviner', a protector in a religious or magical sense.

Dalang are also social commentators. Traditionally, when a travelling dalang arrives at a place where he is to perform, he will make a study of what is on people's minds. That may, for example, be government measures which people find hard to accept. During the performance, the dalang will use the *pånåkawan*, the servants who make humorous and barbed comments, to voice criticism which the audience will relate to. According to tradition, a dalang cannot be held responsible for what is said in his performance. In feudal society one of the dalang's main roles was to be a mouthpiece for the people. His ritual immunity protected him from the wrath of those criticized. However, most of the time, dalangs were diplomatic in the way they said things.

The work of the dalang is difficult because they need to have many talents and obey many regulations. Before they can perform independently, aspiring dalangs are trained for years. That only used to be possible as an apprentice, but since the Sixties there have been schools on Java where young dalangs are trained.

Apart from the professional dalangs, there are also amateurs. Most dalangs in the villages are farmers, while at court, by tradition they are mostly professionals and servants of the court.

Dalangs must conform to a number of court-derived prescriptions and traditions: a) *åntåwacånå* (intonation), to make the distinction between the voice of each character, all of which have their own characteristic voice. The combination of the shape of the eyes and the position of the head determines the register and the sound of each character's voice. A dalang has nine voices for the main figures, as well as the typical language of each one; b) *renggep* (to involve completely), to keep the performance lively; c) *enges* (emotion), to create interest in the characters and involve and move the audience, for instance during a dialogue between lovers; d) *tutug* (eloquence), to recite prescribed dialogues or *pagedongan* (traditional, fixed explanations); e) *banyol* (comedy), to make the audience laugh; f) *sabet* (flow, wave), to handle the puppets correctly, and properly distinguish between the movements of the various wayang puppets, especially during fight scenes; g) *kawiråjå* (*kawi* refers to the old Javanese mode of speech, *råjå* means prince), to be able to recite the traditional eulogy prior to the performance, praising the government, the eminence of the ruling king, and the prosperity of his kingdom; h) *paråmå-kawi* (*paråmå* is the Sanskrit word meaning

high), to correctly explain the nicknames of the kings and nobles in the performance; i) *amardi-båså* (to focus on language), to know the different ways that gods, giants or humans speak in their various social positions (hierarchy is strongly embedded in the Javanese language, which has two completely separate vocabularies: if the listener has a higher status *kråmå* is used, but if he has a low status *ngoko* is used); j) *paråmå-sastrå*, to know the writings *(layang)* on which a performance may be based, and which are necessary to determine the contents of the *suluk* (narrative announcements) and *greget saut* (pieces of music); k) *awicaritå* (knowledge of many tales), to know all the tales referred to in a performance, the character depicted by each puppet, and the significance of each stage requisite; l) *amardåwå-lagu* (melodious singing), to know the verse measures and singing techniques which are used in a performance.

A dalang also needs to observe the following courtly prohibitions: he may not change the form of a performance once it is recorded in the *pakem* (handbooks of the court); he may not show any preference for a character; he may not show himself during a performance, or speak out of turn; he may not focus criticism on anyone, or anger his audience; he may not make uncouth jokes; he must make sure that the performance lasts for the correct duration (from about 7.30 p.m. to 6 a.m.), and that each aspect of the performance lasts the appropriate time.

The ideal dalang therefore has to possess many technical skills and personal qualities. He not only needs to be an excellent performer and religious mediator, but he also has the task of pointing out social ills and making his audience aware of their shortcomings.

Repertoire

Wayang can be seen as a representation of Javanese thought, especially wayang purwå, which has a repertoire that consists of a sizable cycle of tales derived from ancient Indonesian myths and two Indian epics, the Ramayana and the Mahabharata. The Javanese word *purwå* means 'beginning' or 'first', and is probably derived from *parwan*, a Sanskrit word used to denote the chapters of the Mahabharata. These ancient stories about gods, giants and kings form the basis for the different *lakon* and reflect ideas about the cosmic system, in which man is but a small insignificant part, subject to divine and demonic powers.

To understand wayang it is necessary to comprehend this world of gods, demons and humans in which everything is based on good and evil forces: gods on one side, demons and giants on the other. These two parties each have their own topography in the wayang performance: the good come from the right side, the bad from the left. Humans stand between gods and giants and can choose either side. If they wish to join the gods and gain their support, they must prove their suitability by means of long, hard penance. Only a privileged few can attain to a long-standing relationship with the heavenly powers. If they choose the side of the giants, less preparation is needed: no penance and simply obeying the giants is sufficient. By themselves, the gods are powerless to overcome the giants.

The wayang purwå repertoire consists of four different performance cycles. The first, the preamble, deals with the origins of the world and the vicissitudes of the gods, and is inspired by both the Adiparwa, the prologue of the Mahabharata, and ancient Indonesian tales.

The second, the Arjunå Såsrå Bau cycle, deals with the lineage of several prominent characters of the Ramayana, including the birth of the twelve-headed giant known as Rawånå or Dåsåmukå, and his opponent

Left: Ancient giant receiving instruction from a god, 65 and 48 cm, early 19th century, Kraton Kasepuhan, Cirebon, west Java.

93

Arjuna Sasra Bau, he of a thousand arms, an incarnation of the god Wisnu.

The third cycle, the Rama cycle, is based on the Ramayana, and tells the story of the errant hero Rama, who goes in search of his wife, who was kidnapped by the giant known as Rawana or Dasamuka. This story is even more popular on Bali than on Java.

The fourth cycle, the Pandawa cycle, is most popular on Java, and is based on episodes from the Mahabharata, the story of the struggle between the Pandawa and Korawa brothers, which ends with a disastrous battle.

Preamble: stories of the gods

Three groups are brought on stage whose colourful deeds will fill the *lakon*: the gods in heaven, their enemies – the giants of 'the other side' – and the humans. From the outset, the gods and giants are enemies vying for power. The giants, reminiscent of the Titans of Greek mythology, repeatedly try to seize a heavenly nymph, and the gods beat a retreat before the giants' furious onslaught. Usually 'a man of great strength' is needed to force the giants into retreat and to save the threatened abode of the gods, the Suralaya, from the powerful enemy.

The distance between gods and men is not so great in this primeval setting, and this causes much trouble. Although the gods possess divine power, they show the same weaknesses as the humans living on earth. Moreover, humans can obtain an almost godlike spiritual power by practising *tapa* (meditation) and *semadi* (asceticism).

Some stories in the preamble relate the good deeds of the gods for the humans, e.g. the tale of the origin of crops (especially rice) and the harmful influences to which they are prone, and the ways in which evil can be countered; it relates the forging of the first weapons, and the use of animals in the fields.

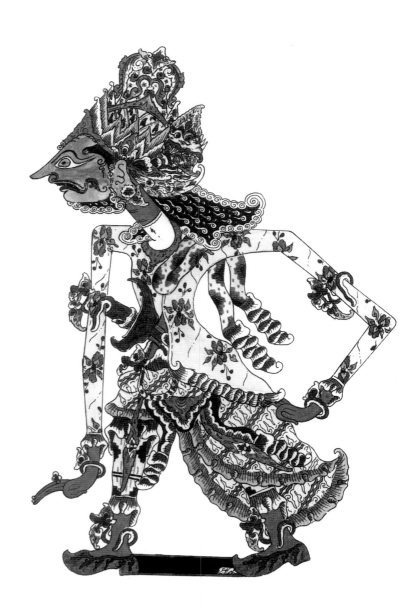

Creation: the gods in the Surålåyå

The Supreme Being Wiseså (Hyang Tunggal) originated from chaos.
Heaven, earth, sun, moon and the two gods Manik and Måyå came into
existence next. The youngest of the two brothers, Manik, or Baṭårå
Guru, became Wiseså's successor and lives in the Surålåyå, the abode of
the gods. The eldest, the black and deformed Måyå (or Ismåyå or Baṭårå
Semar), was banished to earth and ordered to assist the descendants of
the gods who live there, the Pandåwå.

The Supreme god, Baṭårå Guru (which means Divine Teacher), rules
over the Surålåyå, populated by nymphs and gods. He has many sons.
The most important are Baṭårå Endrå, guardian of the abode of the
gods, Baṭårå Bayu, god of the winds, Baṭårå Kålå, god of evil, and
Baṭårå Bråmå, god of fire and opponent of Baṭårå Wisnu.

Baṭårå Wisnu is reincarnated on earth five times, and features in
every cycle of the purwå repertoire: as King Arjunå Såsrå Bau of
Maespati and, simultaneously, as his prime minister, Patih Suwåndå, he
is the opponent of the fierce demon King Rawånå (also called
Dåsåmukå). As Råmå, main character in the Råmå cycle, he is the opponent of the giant Dåsåmukå (or Rawånå) once again. He is also incarnated as the hero Arjunå, the middle of the Pandåwå brothers, and as
King Kresnå of Dwåråwati, who also appears in the Pandåwå cycle.

The beautiful wife of Baṭårå Guru is Baṭari Durgå who, because of a
curse, changes into Baṭari Umå, the ugly and evil goddess, and becomes
the wife of Baṭårå Kålå.

The sons of Ismåyå are Baṭårå Kåmåjåyå, the god of love, (his wife
Dewi Kåmåratih is the goddess of love), Baṭårå Yåmådipati, god of the
realm of the dead, and Baṭårå Suryå, the sun god.

Dewi Ngruni and Dewi Ngrunå and the Birth of the *Garuḍås* and *Någås*

Baṭårå Suryå, god of the sun, is husband to two nymphs, Dewi Ngrunå and Dewi Ngruni. They were given two eggs as a gift. The eggs are hatched by a large snake, and out of Dewi Ngrunå's eggs come two *garuḍås*: Sempati and Jatayu. Many snakes come out of Dewi Ngruni's egg.

As a result of an argument between the two nymphs, Dewi Ngruni is changed into a giantess. One day, when the Surålåyå is threatened by the army of a giant king, Wisnu dispatches giantess Ngruni to kidnap the king's daughter and *Garuḍå* Jatayu is sent to attack the giant army. The giants are defeated. As a reward, *Garuḍå* Jatayu is given the kidnapped giant princess as his wife, and Dewi Ngruni is changed back into a nymph by Wisnu. She is so grateful for this that she wants to stay with him, but on Baṭårå Guru's orders she returns to her husband Baṭårå Suryå.

Dewi Sintå and her son Watugunung

Dewi Sintå is the second wife of a king. Feeling humiliated, she leaves the court when she becomes pregnant. As a result, her son is born in the woods. One day, in a rage, she hits the child over the head with a rice spoon, causing a scar. He flees, and Dewi Sintå never hears from him again. Many years later, when he is crowned King Watugunung of Gilingwesi, he falls in love with a princess and marries her without realising that she is his own mother.

One day, Dewi Sintå notices the scar on his head and realises what she has done. She advises her son and husband to marry a nymph from Surålåyå, the residence of the gods. He is denied entrance by Baṭårå Endrå, the guard. When Watugunung threatens to kidnap the girl with his army, Baṭårå Endrå calls for the assistance of Putut Jantåkå, the mighty hermit. In the struggle that ensues, Watugunung is killed and, with his death, Sintå's disgrace is dissolved and harmony is restored on earth.

Dewi Sri, goddess of agriculture

One of the most important gods is Dewi Sri. She is the goddess of agriculture, the goddess of rice, and therefore also the symbol of fertility. *Lakon* in which she is the subject are performed on the occasion of the rice harvest and *bersih-deså* (the annual cleansing of the village) to chase away evil forces.

During the reign of King Mengukuhan of Mendangkamulan, Batårå Wisnu and Dewi Sri descend to earth. They are incarnated as the king and his queen, Tisnåwati. When Tisnåwati dies, all kinds of beneficial crops grow from her interred body: rice grows from her eyes, coconut palm from her head, various kinds of bamboo from her thighs, and sugar palm from her vagina. Even in these vegetal forms she cannot escape Kålågumarang, Batårå Kålå's son. He hunted her when she was still a celestial being, and, since he was changed into a swine, he now damages the fields. Batårå Wisnu finally kills him with an arrow, but insects and injurious plant diseases spring up from Kålågumarang's body. Moreover, Kålågumarang's evil soul alters many humans into harmful forest animals such as pigs, rats, apes, cows, and buffalo. These plagues are eventually overcome using magic, except for the cows and buffalo: from now on these animals will be useful to the farmers.

King Måhåpunggung of Mendangkamulan has a son and a daughter: Jåkå Sedånå, a terrestrial manifestation of Wisnu, and Dewi Sri. Jåkå Sedånå suddenly disappears from court, causing a great stir. Then Kålå Daru makes his appearance, sent as a messenger by the demon King Pulågrå to ask for the hand of the princess. Dewi Sri flatly refuses and declares that she will only marry someone who is equal to her brother in every respect. Thereupon her father banishes her to the forests. During her ramble Dewi Sri meets friendly peasants who lend her hospitality, but Kålå Daru appears and Dewi Sri flees hurriedly away. Nature is in chaos and commotion, a fact which is noted in the abode of the gods. Batårå Nårådå is sent to tell her the hiding place of her brother Jåkå Sedånå, who remains stubborn in his refusal to return to his father's kingdom before his sister is married. Unexpectedly, Dewi Sri stands before him, and a moment later the feared Kålå Daru also appears. Jåkå Sedånå scares the loathsome demon away, and brother and sister decide to begin a new life in the forest of Medangagung. They collect the seeds of all kinds of agricultural crops, including coconut, rice, cassava, red pepper, eggplant and maize. While busy preparing the fields, the demon King Pulågrå suddenly arrives with his army. The resulting bustle stirs even the abode of the gods. It is Batårå Bayu who eventually succeeds in dislodging all the demons by blowing an enormous gale. Batårå Narådå wants the siblings to marry in the presence of all the gods, but they decline. Jåkå Sedånå is then banished from Java.

Batårå Kålå

The evil that threatens man is personified in Batårå Kålå, a son of Batårå Guru. Batårå Kålå was conceived from the sperm of Batårå Guru, which accidentally fell into the ocean as he chased a princess who was practising asceticism in the middle of the waters. She fled from his amorous approaches, and the sperm developed into a demonic being who is banned to the world of mortals. Batårå Kålå's father gave him permission to eat certain mortals, known as *wong sukertå*, people who are under the influence of evil, and who thus run the risk of falling prey for Kålå's appetite. Batårå Guru's consort is Batari Durgå. She was once a beautiful goddess, but was transformed into a dangerous female demon by a curse, and became notorious for her black magic. She appropriates those who made certain mistakes in their households – such as knocking over a steam kettle for rice as it is cooking – as prey for Batårå Kålå. After Batårå Kålå has left the abode of the gods, Batårå Guru regrets giving his consent to Batårå Kålå. Batårå Narådå, the divine messenger, comes up with a stratagem: magic spells are written on Kålå's head, body, arms and hands, and whenever these spells are read aloud, Kålå's power over the *wong sukertå* disappears. Batårå Kålå is told that the spells will make it clear to whoever reads them that he is Batårå Guru's son. The gods Batårå Guru (Wisnu in some versions of the story), Narådå, and Bråmå descend to earth and pose as wayang performers. However, the performance is disturbed by Batårå Kålå, who is chasing *wong sukertå*, in this case a boy and a girl who have lost their brothers or sisters. When the frightened children hide between the *gamelan* instruments, Batårå Kålå challenges the dalang, but when the divine dalang starts reading the spells from Kålå's body, Kålå has to concede that the dalang is older and more powerful. He loses his powers and is forced to promise to leave the *wong sukertå* alone and make do with some of the sacrificial food. Batårå Kålå disappears into thin air.

The only way to cleanse people who are *wong sukertå* is by organizing a *ruwat* ceremony. Only the senior dalang, descended from families with a long dalang tradition, are qualified to give a *ruwat* performance, because only they can control the strong evil powers that are brought to life in the person of Batårå Kålå. At the end of the performance, the dalang dips the sticks of the wayang puppets in holy water so that the powers of the gods can flow into the water. The person for whom the performance was given is then washed with this water to wash away the evil spell that made him *wong sukertå*.

Page 106: Monster resembling a rhinoceros, 64 cm, c. 1960, Arjawinangun, Cirebon, west Java. Together with other traditional centres for ceremonies and the arts such as the *kratons* (Sultan's courts), and the communities of Plumbon, Trusmi, Gegesik and Indramayu, Arjawinangun is remarkable because it has preserved its specific character in the theatrical arts. This is based on a strong and continuous blend of the overlapping cultures that have influenced these coastal and inland regions. At first there was animism, ancestor worship, Hinduism, Buddhism, and Islam. Later on, 'modern' 20th-century ideas such as nationalism, literacy, school-based education, independency, and so forth came along. Among the extensive collection of theatre puppets once owned by this Arjawinangun dalang there is a relatively high number which bear the characteristics of a swamp or water monster. These wayang all are scaly and have short-limbed claws on which one can imagine them moving through shallows. They look like evil relatives of the mythical snake Nägä. Sometimes they even bear distinguishing marks of the awesome devil himself. At the end of the 19th century, there were still rhinoceroses in west Java.

Page 107: Two demons, 43 and 49 cm, c. 1850 or later, Kraton Kasepuhan, Cirebon, west Java. The devil on the left has an umbilical hernia. They represent incarnations of bringers of plagues that befall mankind in times of war or other difficult times, such as famine or crop failure. These spiteful figures are harbingers of dysentery or cholera epidemics, miscarriage, or other kinds of sickness that threaten families. The dreaded demons are considered to lurk in wait for men to fail to behave as expected by the fickle spirits from the netherworld, or when they fail to bring enough proper offerings. Sometimes the figures are made from horrifying materials such as the skin of a murdered person, or the skin of a woman who died in childbirth. It is said that this skin must be stolen from the corpse before or shortly after burial.

The Arjunå Såsrå Bau cycle

The Arjunå Såsrå Bau cycle is mainly about giants. The main character
in these *lakon* is Rawånå or Dåsåmukå, the evil ten-headed giant who,
after becoming king of Alengkå (Sri Lanka), is defeated by Arjunå Såsrå
Bau, an incarnation of Arjunå. The fearsome Dåsåmukå has two brothers
and one sister: the giants Kumbåkarnå and Wibisånå, and the giantess
Sarpåkenåkå. After a long period practising asceticism on Mount
Gohkarnå, the inner strength of the merciless giant Dåsåmukå has
become so great that even the gods are so afraid of him that they grant
his every wish. Dåsåmukå thus succeeds in gaining power over heaven
and earth and, once he has become invincible, he goes about commit-
ting many misdeeds without let or hindrance. When he is crowned king
of Ngalengkå, he wants Dewi Widawati, an incarnation of Dewi Sri, to
be his wife. However, he encounters a strong opponent: the incarnation
of Wisnu who, in the guise of Arjunå Såsrå Bau, defeats Dåsåmukå but
allows him to live, on the condition that he subjugate himself to Arjunå.
In all the adventures in this cycle, Dåsåmukå remains the opponent of
Arjunå Såsrå Bau. Both assume the supernatural, terrifying appearance
of Brahålå by practising *triwikråmå*. Arjunå succeeds in defeating the
giant each time, but then he meets the wise giant Råmå Parasu, who
possesses the Bargåwastrå, a holy bow and arrow of gigantic propor-
tions. Råmå challenges Arjunå Såsrå Bau to draw it, and he is succeed-
ing until suddenly it snaps and kills him. The ten-headed, twenty-armed
Dåsåmukå is free to revert to his evil ways.

The tales from the Arjunå Såsrå Bau cycle are linked to the tales of
the Råmå cycle, as the figures in the Arjunå Såsrå Bau cycle are the
ancestors of characters in later stories, and the origins of conflicts in the
later stories are explained. For example, when Råmå meets the monkey
king Sugriwå, who is in conflict with his brother Subali, much of the
dispute has already been explained in the Arjunå Såsrå Bau cycle.
Dåsåmukå and his brothers and Wibisånå, and their sister, the giantess
Sarpåkenåkå, also figure in the Råmå cycle.

L.W.

Page 112: Young demon, 65.5 cm, c. 1850 or older, Pasisir, north coast of Java. The young giant, probably an army commander, wears his hair in a knot with a diadem. Demons like this one are sure to cause the audience to roar with laughter because of their stupidity, and they are thus very popular on stage.

Left above: Prince Kångså, 62.5 cm, 19th century, Yogyakarta, central Java. This puppet may also be used as an 'enemy king'. The *doḍot* (ceremonial robe) that he is wearing bears the princely motif *parang rusak* in red, as befits the status of this powerful half-demon, the son of demon King Goråwångså. Goråwångså was infatuated with Dewi Maerah, King Basudewå's queen. He took the form of her husband and impregnated the unknowing Dewi Maerah, who was then exiled to the jungle by her husband. When Kångså reached maturity, he went to Madurå and asked for the kingdom. By his extraordinary magical powers he succeeded in having his wish granted. At the same time he sought to kill Kakrasånå and Nåråyånå, the sons of King Basudewå. The twin princes were still children, and not strong enough to resist the demon king effectively. Because of this danger their father hid them by disguising them. To lure them into the open, Kångså then held a contest. The two brothers contrived to defeat their enemy in the ensuing fight.

Left below: Demon-prince, 58.5 cm, c. 1900 or later, Pasisir, north coast of Java. The winged ornament on the back of this youthful army commander is a *pråbå* (aureole). The way wayang are dressed mirrors the style of dress at the Javanese courts of the Mataram period (c. 1650-c. 1750). In wayang stories portrayed by dancers, costumes of the same type are used, and during marriage festivities, according to long-standing custom, bride and groom are dressed as 'king and queen (for a day)' or as 'ancestors'. In many cases this means that they are dressed like wayang figures. In that case, the groom may wear a crown and other jewellery around his neck, arms, and ankles, but he will not wear the wing-like ornament on his back as shown here, which actually represents an aureole as a sign of the prince's status and qualities.

The Råmå cycle

In this cycle, the leader of the giants is again King Dåsåmukå (Rawånå) of Ngalengkå. He now goes so far as to kidnap Råmå's wife, and this leads to the demise of Dåsåmukå. In this way, Wisnu, who has come to earth as Råmå, puts an end to the giant by killing him, which he did not manage in the Ajunå Såsrå Bau cycle.

While meditating on a mountain, Dåsåråtå meets Princess Dewi Ragu, who has fled from the giant Rawånå or Dåsåmukå. They marry, and when her father is killed by the giant, Dåsåråtå becomes king of Ngayojå. Dewi Ragu gives birth to their eldest son Råmå (called Regåwå in his youth), in whom Wisnu is incarnated. It is in this form that Wisnu will fight and vanquish the giant king of Ngalengkå. (Dåsåråtå has his sons, Lesmånå, Baråtå and Satrugnå by his other wives)

Råmå vanquished the giants at the request of the holy hermit Yogiswårå. They had been coming to devour the daily sacrifices for some time, and threatened to destroy the hermitage. The grateful hermit advises the young prince to go to Mantili, where a *sayembårå* is to be held for Princess Sintå. Råmå wins the archery contest and weds Sintå. She is an incarnation of Dewi Sri and predestined to marry Råmå.

Old King Dåsåråtå had appointed Råmå as his successor. However, when preparations are being made for the coronation, his jealous second wife Kekayi rebels because she wants her own son Baråtå, Råmå's younger brother, to be king. She presses her husband to crown Baråtå instead of Råmå, and reminds him of a promise he made long ago to fulfil her every desire. Dåsåråtå cannot break his word, and fulfils Kekayi's wish with a heavy heart. Soon afterwards he dies of grief. Råmå goes into exile without protest to honour his father's word. He only permits his wife Sintå and his devoted brother Lesmånå to accompany him.

After an exhausting journey they reach the village of Citråkutå, where they settle. There they are found by Baråtå, who was ignorant of

Right: Råmå and Sintå in royal dress, 48.5 and 35.5 cm, late 19th century, Cirebon, west Java. Råmå and Sintå are incarnations of the god Wisnu and his spouse Dewi Sri. These two gods also appear in other incarnations: Wisnu as Kresnå and Arjunå; Dewi Sri as Dewi Sumbådrå. Later on, Javanese kings and their queens were also regarded as manifestations of Wisnu and Sri. To this very day, each betrothed couple on Java is seen as representations of these gods on the day of their marriage.

his mother's machinations, and begs Râmâ to take his place on the throne. Râmâ refuses and sends his brother home. But Barâtâ takes Râmâ's sandals to put them on the throne. This gesture legitimizes Barâtâ as Râmâ's deputy in the eyes of the people. Râmâ treks deeper into the forest with Sintâ and Lesmânâ, out of reach of his family and people. They finally end their flight in the forest of Pâncâwati, where the brothers build a hut.

One day, while she is roaming the forest, the giantess Sarpâkenâkâ, Dâsâmukâ's sister, runs into Râmâ. She falls in love with him at first sight. Râmâ rejects her advances, and the lovesick giantess then directs her affections to Lesmânâ, who is as unenthusiastic as his brother. When Sarpâkenâkâ persists, he mutilates her nose and ears in disgust.

Deeply hurt and vengeful, Sarpâkenâkâ goes to her brother for help. In her twisted way, she tells him of her humiliation, and she cleverly tells Dâsâmukâ about Sintâ's beauty. Dâsâmukâ orders his servant Maricâ to transform himself into a golden deer to entice Sintâ.

Sintâ catches sight of the animal but fails to catch it. She begs her husband to get it for her. At first Râmâ is suspicious, but eventually he gives in to his wife's entreaties and goes out with his bow, making Lesmânâ promise not to leave his wife by herself. Suddenly Sintâ and Lesmânâ are startled by a voice like Râmâ's calling for help. Sintâ is out of her mind with worry and, in her delusion she forces Lesmânâ to leave her and find the supposed Râmâ. Now Rawânâ himself appears, disguised as a wandering monk. He violently takes Sintâ up into the sky, where *Garuda* Jatayu, an old friend of Râmâ's father, hears Sintâ's cries for help and attacks Rawânâ. Jatayu is fatally wounded and falls to the ground, but before he dies he tells Râmâ and Lesmânâ about Sintâ's abduction.

Stricken by grief, the two brothers search the forest and the fields, hoping to find some trace of Sintâ. Râmâ is able to help the monkey king Sugriwâ, whose wife and kingdom were taken by his brother Subali. Finding themselves in similar situations, Râmâ and Sugriwâ are consolidated and they promise to help each other as best they can.

During a fight between Sugriwå and Subali, Råmå kills Subali with an arrow, and the grateful monkey king, all his powers restored, puts his army and his people at Råmå's disposal to help free Sintå. Sugriwå orders his best general, Hanuman, to find Sintå. Hanuman takes a flying leap (his father is Bayu, the god of the winds) and lands on the other side of the ocean, and proceeds to the capital of Ngalengkå. In the garden of Ngargåsokå he finds the despondent Sintå. Hidden in a tree, he sees how Sintå rejects Rawånå's advances and threatens to commit suicide if he comes too close.

When the giant king leaves, Hanuman (who was barely able to contain himself) makes himself known to Sintå as her husband's envoy and gives her Råmå's ring. To test the enemy's strength he starts destroying the garden, and fights the guards who come running in. The monkey finally allows himself to be taken prisoner and is brought before the king in chains. At first the king wants to kill him right away, but at the entreaty of his brothers, Kumbåkarnå and Wibisånå, who have more noble characters, Rawånå spares Hanuman because of his ambassadorial status. Nonetheless, Rawånå wishes to punish the monkey for his effrontery. He orders the monkey to be wrapped in combustible rags and then sets fire to him. However, Hanuman manages to escape and, with his tail on fire, he joyously jumps over the houses of the city and sets fire to everything in his path. The fire cannot harm him and, with a terrific flying leap, he returns home. After he has made his report, it is clear to Råmå and Sugriwå what they must do: on to Ngalengkå! To get across the ocean, the monkey army, helped by fish and other creatures of the sea, builds a dam of boulders across to the island. The army crosses over and heads for the capital, where a bloody battle with the giants ensues. On the enemy side, one of the chief champions is the king's brother, the terrible Kumbåkarnå, who has a noble character in spite of his being a giant. He is prepared to die for king and country, even though he does not agree with fighting a war over a wife.

Wibisånå, Rawånå's other brother, looks like a human, and defects to Råmå's army. He elevates justice, which is not bound to countries,

117

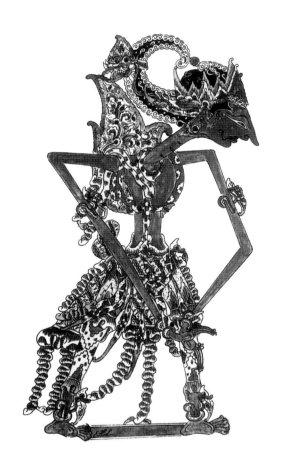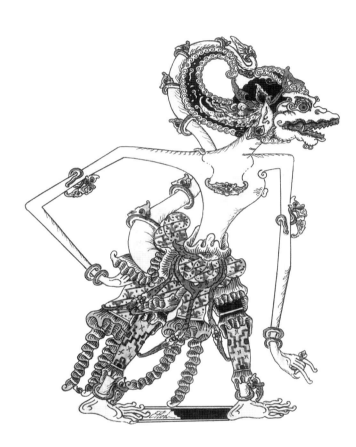

above faith to his country. Kumbåkarnå likes to wear white on the battlefield, like someone doomed to die. He dies at the hand of Lesmånå after inflicting a lot of damage. Now, having lost his best warriors, Rawånå himself joins the battle. He finds Råmå opposite him. The battle between the two heroes is terrific. Although Råmå beheads Rawånå with his mighty arrow, kyai Gruwå Wijånå, the giant is not killed. Rawånå's head immediately re-attaches itself by magic. Hanuman the monkey is ordered to throw a mountain onto Rawånå's body the second time it is beheaded, until the head is seperated from the trunk forever.

Sintå is liberated, but the reunification with Råmå is not so easy. In the presence of all, Råmå declares that his victory has avenged the injury done to him, but a woman who has belonged to another can no longer be his wife, so he divorces Sintå.

Sintå, for whom life has lost all meaning, asks to be burned to death, but the high flames do not hurt her. The fire god Agni appears, and returns Sintå to her husband with the assurance that she has always remained faithful. All are greatly touched when the reconciliation finally takes place. Råmå, Sintå and Lesmånå then return to Ngayojå, where the faithful Baråtå receives them with joy and Råmå is crowned king.

After the happy end to this story, there is another chapter which was probably not part of the original epic. There is no *lakon* extant concerning these later episodes. One day, Råmå learns that in spite of the trial by fire, his subjects do not approve of his taking back Sintå. People think that his taking back a wife from another man sets the wrong example. Råmå then banishes loyal Sintå, who is received into the hermitage of Walmiki the wise, where she gives birth to the twins, Låwå and Kuså. The boys grow up under the guidance of the hermit and their mother. Years later they hear the rumour that King Råmå will make the great horse sacrifice. The hermit goes to the city with the two boys to witness the event, and the boys, as accomplished singers, sing a chapter of the Råmåyana which the hermit had taught them every day. Their fame spreads, and the boys are summoned to the throne. When Råmå learns that the boys are Sintå's sons, he has their mother brought in and commands her to swear an oath in front of everyone to cleanse her of the suspicion that still clung to her. The much-maligned lady invokes the earth to swallow her if she has loved anyone other than her husband Råmå. Then the earth swallows Sintå. Råmå vainly begs the earth to return his wife. A long time later, Råmå is admitted to heaven, where he reigns as Wisnu again.

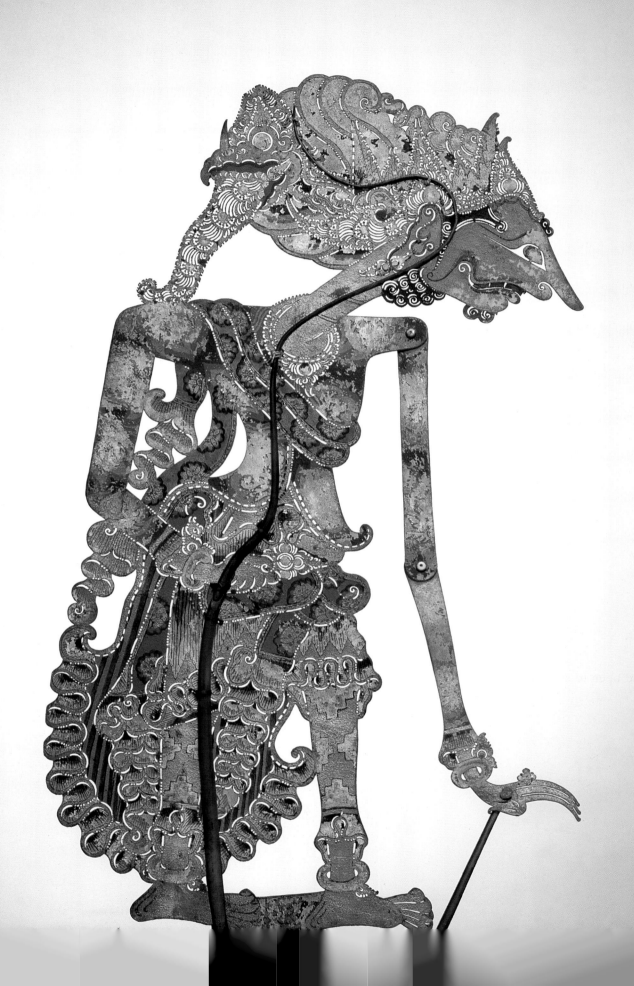

The Pandåwå Cycle

In the Pandåwå cycle, humans, rather than gods or giants, come to the fore. Prospering realms have been founded on Java, only to be ruined by the shortcomings of their rulers. The story of the Mahabharata is very complicated and involves many kingdoms and characters from different generations of several families. However, the main theme is the struggle between the Pandåwå and the Koråwå, between good and evil. These families are descendants of the founders of the realm of Astinå, whose divine ancestors were children of the gods Bråmå and Wisnu. Their struggle can be seen as a struggle between good and evil: one group, the five Pandåwå brothers, helps the gods and is supported by them, while the other, the ninety-nine Koråwå brothers, has close links with the 'giants of the other side'.

Abiåså, the old king of Astinå, has two sons. The eldest, Dåstårastrå, was born blind and is the father of one hundred children, the Koråwå: ninety-nine sons and one daughter. Abiåså's younger son, Pandu, is the father of five sons, the Pandåwå.

Yudistirå is the oldest of the five Pandåwå, and represents the purest example of a good king. His own wishes always take second place to those of others, however negligible those might be. His only weapon is a sympathetic heart. Darmå, the god of justice, is his spiritual father.

Bimå, the second of the Pandåwå, posesses gargantuan strength, and displays incomparable bravery and assuredness. He is merciless, takes on every challenge, is tempestuous and temperamental, honest and open to an embarrassing degree, but also infallibly true to those he loves. Bayu, the god of the winds, is his spiritual father.

Arjunå, the third of the Pandåwå, is quite different. For the older Javanese he represents the perfect man: finely built yet an unequalled warrior, and as beautiful and elegant as a woman. He is capable of the strictest self-discipline, in spite of his many wives and mistresses. He is

Left: King Abiåså as a hermit, 48 cm, c. 1850 or older, north coast of Java. King Abiåså is the grandfather of the Pandåwå and Koråwå, to whom the authorship of the whole Mahabharata epic is attributed. After the great battle, the Pandåwå and their associates were sitting together in their deep dejection when he 'appeared to the discouraged group mysteriously, as if out of nowhere' and said: "The reason for my visit is to admonish you in your grief and distress. Extinguish this mood with the correct insight...your remembrance of the deepest wisdom shall serve to cleanse you of your troubled hearts...The battle and death therein is truly by Syiwa's decree...Therefore you must simply acquiesce to the fact that I believe that those who follow the *dharma* in the fight shall find their resting place in the heavens...[the] death [of thy sons] shall bear fruit, take comfort in this. Whoever needs to be reassured of the truth of my words will receive my supernatural vision, with which you will be able to see momentarily." Thus spake Wyasa to the deeply distressed group. They all made a *sembah* (reverent salute), and eventually they were comforted in their sorrow, because they were given insight in the circumstance of all the vanquished. They even saw into the past and the future in the three worlds.'

the calm lover of life, forgiving the slights done to him by his cousins because they are family, but entering into battle with them with a heavy heart because his duty as *satriå* (a nobleman) requires it. His spiritual father is Indrå, the rain god.

The two youngest Pandåwå, the twins Nakulå and Sadewå, are sons of Pandu's second wife Madrim, but they are raised together with the other three Pandåwå by Dewi Kunti, Pandu's first wife. Nakulå and Sadewå are descended from two gods of light, the Aswin.

When King Abiåså has reached old age, he abdicates and retreats to live as a hermit on mount Retawu. The gods give him the power to see the future and become very old. Tragically, he will live long enough to see the final disastrous battle between his own offspring, the Koråwå and the Pandåwå.

Because an invalid king was unacceptable, and would have an adverse effect on the kingdom and its people, Pandu rules as a regent for Dåstårastrå.

Their children are raised together. The ninety-nine Koråwå brothers and their sister, and the five Pandåwå brothers are educated by their great-uncle, Bimå the hero, and Durnå, the wise brahmin. As children, the Pandåwå show their superiority over their cousins in a ceaseless

Page 124: Dewi Kunti and the prelate of Sokålimå, sage Durnå, 35 and 46.5 cm, c. 1850, Kraton Kasepuhan, Cirebon, west Java. Kunti, mother of the Pandåwå, is wearing a long *kebaya* with a *selendang* (shoulder cloth) on a *kain* or *sarung* with the *parang rusak* motif, which is only worn by royalty. Long *kebaya*'s are rarely worn in wayang, but if they are, only by elderly ladies like Dewi Kunti. One day, Princess Kunti – still a young girl – repaired to the river, when the day was at its hottest and the sun at its highest point in the heavens, in order to take a refreshing bathe. This trip was to be her downfall: the sun god Suryå noticed her beauty and impregnated her with his rays. The princess bore a child, who was to become the king of Awangga, at a place far from the court. In order not to jeopardise her future, the sun god made sure that Kunti's child was brought into the world via Kunti's *karnå* (ear), and thus was the boy given this name. He was raised by a charioteer and his wife. When he reached adulthood he took his place on the side of the Koråwå.

Later, Kunti married king Pandu, and had three more sons: Yudistirå, Bimå and Arjunå. In their youth the princes were raised by Durnå the wise, along with their cousins, the Koråwå. One of the things he taught them was military skills. Durnå, adviser of the king and nestor of the Koråwå side, was greatly respected by his pupils. But he is biased; his favourite Arjunå was given preferential treatment at the expense of the others. Indeed, he is called the 'Macchiavelli' of wayang because of his cunning. Durnå is dressed as a spiritual leader or god: a headcloth, and a shoulder cloth on a long coat, called *jubah*. He is also wearing shorts on top of a pair of long trousers. Another sign of his spiritual status are his shoes, which are only worn by gods or important priests in wayang.

Above left: Dåstårastrå, the blind king, father of the Koråwå, eldest son of King Abiåså of Astinå.

Above right: Pandu, the pale-skinned father of the Pandåwå, younger son of King Abiåså.

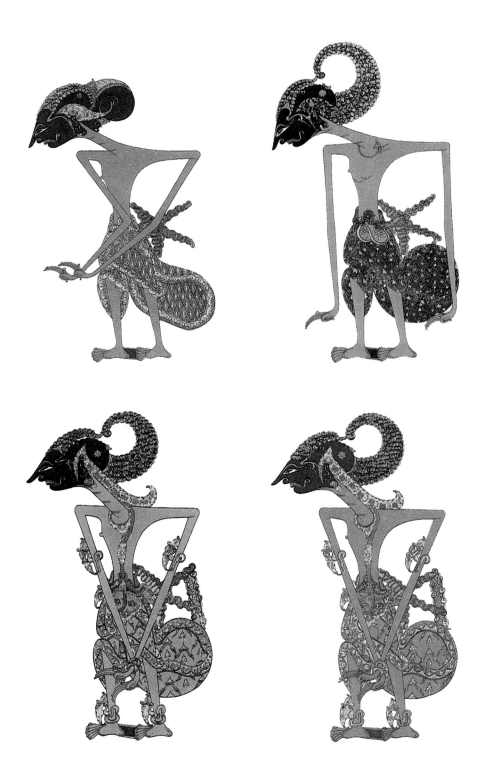

The five Pandåwå:

Page 126: Bimå, a giant fighting injustice.

Left, clockwise: Yudistirå, the just king of Amartå;
Arjuná, the noble hero; the twins Nakulá and
Sadewå.

Four of the five brothers wear their hair in a *supit
urang*, curled upwards, with a smaller curl on their
forehead curled backwards. Only the eldest,
Yudistirå, wears his hair in a bun, the *gelung
keling*. All brothers wear a *kain bokongan* tucked
up in front, with a bulging posterior, and have their
feet close to each other.

Their nobility is obvious: their faces are directed
downwards and their facial colours are black, gold
or white. Although also a nobleman, the features of
the giant Bimá are slightly different because he is
the spiritual son of Batårå Bayu, god of the winds.
He is well-built and has round eyes, a large pro-
truding nose, and a sharp thumbnail with which he
can kill an enemy instantly. He is dressed in the
sacred *kain poleng*, a black and white, checkered
loincloth.

rivalry, for which they come to be hated by the Koråwå. This rancour deepens when, after regent Pandu's death, the old, blind King Dåstårastrå appoints his eldest nephew, Yudistirå, as successor to the throne. This infuriates the Koråwå, especially the first-born, remorseless Suyudånå, and they plan to destroy the Pandåwå.

Under the guise of friendship, the Pandåwå are given a specially built guesthouse during a visit to the capital city of Ngastinapurå. But this 'house of lacquer' burns easily and, during the night, the brothers barely escape a fiery death by fleeing through an underground passageway. The Pandåwå are then exiled from Astinå for good.

After many adventures, they enter into the service of King Matswapati of Wiråtå. When the king's brother-in-law tries to overthrow him, the five Pandåwå come to his aid and defeat the disloyal man. As a reward, King Matswapati gives them a piece of land in a forest called Wanamarta. This is where the five Pandåwå establish a new realm called Amartå. The oldest of the five brothers, Yudistirå, becomes king.

When the Pandåwå hear that King Drupada of Campala has decreed that a *sayembarå* (archery contest) be held, whose winner will take the hand of Princess Drupadi, they set out for Campala. Arjunå beats all his rivals in archery and, as ancient custom dictates, the princess becomes the husband of all five brothers, although when the four youngest brothers have their own wives, she is mainly associated with Yudistira. Arjunå later marries Sumbådrå, a sister of King Kresnå of Dwarawati, and they have a son, Abimanyu the gentle.

During their travels through the forests, Bimå meets a giant princess whom he marries and who bears him a son, Gatotkåcå the hero. The son inherits his mother's ability to fly and his father's strength and loyalty. He is smaller and more attractive than his father, and also has a stronger character. He is devoted and infallibly loyal to his country, which is typical of the Pandåwå.

Having found powerful allies in Arjunå's father and brother-in-law, King Drupada and King Kresnå of Dwarawati, an incarnation of Wisnu, the Pandawa return to their country. There they find the Koråwå ready

Right: Cakil and Arjunå, 54.5 and 48 cm, late 19th century, Yogyakarta, central Java. Arjunå battling with the demon Cakil at the *perang kembang*, one of the highlights in a wayang performance, which takes place shortly after midnight. Whenever Arjunå or his son Abimanyu are main characters in a wayang purwå play, Cakil is the army commander of the opposing party.

Page 130/131: Suyudǎnǎ and Durnǎ, 58 and
42.5 cm, c. 1960, Surakarta, central Java.
Suyudǎnǎ, the eldest of the Korǎwǎ, with his
teacher and adviser, Durnǎ. His whole life
Suyudǎnǎ suffers from feeling less favoured by the
gods than the Pandǎwǎ brothers and indeed he and
his brothers appear to be less fortunate. Even his
wife, Queen Banowati, has lost her heart to Arjunǎ
as a young girl, and her whole life she maintains a
very close relationship with him. Despite all set
backs, Suyudǎnǎ's behaviour is that of a king. His
face and hands are black as a sign of his high-
strung inner powers. In his hands he holds prayer
beads.

to share the country with them. The Korǎwǎ keep the rich eastern part
and the capital, Ngastinǎpurǎ, while the Pandǎwǎ take the less densely-
populated western part, where they build their new capital, Ngamartǎ.
However, the Korǎwǎ have not given up their plans to possess the
entire kingdom and to wipe out the Pandǎwǎ. On the advice of the
clever Sakuni, an evil genius and counsellor to King Suyudǎnǎ, the
eldest of the ninety-nine Korǎwǎ organizes a peaceful family gathering
and a game of dice, inviting Yudistirǎ, whose only weakness is his
addiction to gambling.

The Korǎwǎ succeed in their plan: once he has started playing, the
normally so temperate Yudistirǎ loses all sense of proportion and plays
away all his property, his kingdom and finally his own freedom, as well
as that of his brothers and his wife, Drupadi. Through the intervention
of the Korǎwǎ's father, the old blind King Dǎstǎrastrǎ, a twelve-year
exile is substituted for enslavement. During this time the Pandǎwǎ must
stay in hiding, and then live for a whole year among the people without
being recognized – if they are noticed, a new period of exile will begin.
After twelve years in the forests the Pandǎwǎ find employment under
false names with King Matswǎpati of Wirǎtǎ. Yudistirǎ plays the part of
the consummate gambler and is taken on to keep the king company.
Bimǎ finds work as a cook in the kitchen, and, as a eunuch, Arjunǎ
becomes the princess' singing and dancing teacher. Nakulǎ becomes a
stable boy, and Sadewǎ herds the king's cows. During this period,
Arjunǎ has retreated as a hermit on Mount Endrakilǎ, where he practises
asceticism and is tested by the gods.

They succeed in not being recognized during the whole period.
Although the Pandǎwǎ have completed their part of the bargain, the
Korǎwǎ refuse to give them even 'as much land as can be covered by
the tip of a needle'. After consultation with their ally and adviser King
Kresnǎ, the Pandǎwǎ decide to use violence to take what is theirs. The
long, violent, final battle, called the Brǎtǎyudǎ, is about to take place.

In the meantime, a new character has been introduced. It is Karnǎ,
the half-brother of the oldest three Pandǎwǎ, the cast-off son of Pandu's

wife, Kunti. He was conceived by the sun god Suryå, who touched Kunti with his sun beams when she was bathing. Karnå's qualities are equal to those of Arjunå: beauty, moral rectitude and heroism. In the beginning, Karnå is not aware of his lineage and is raised by a coach-man's family (in the Javanese version by the king of Petåpralåyå). Later he joins the Koråwå, and in the final battle he shows himself a worthy opponent for Arjunå. The requirements of his *satriå* (nobility) oblige his faithfulness to the Koråwå king, Suyudånå, even though he knows that the Koråwå are unjust in their dealings with their cousins.

Kunti visits him on the eve of the Bråtåyudå (big battle) and begs him not to hurt her sons, the Pandåwå, and to leave the Koråwå. Karnå rebuts her with a reproach that she could never have imagined, and tells her that it is King Suyudånå who has made him what he is now and, as *satriå*, he is required to be loyal. In spite of this, he promises Kunti that he will fight only one of the Pandåwå on the battlefield, Arjunå, who is his equal in so many ways.

The battle is the climax of the story, the epic battle of the descen-dants of Bharåtå. The slaughter goes on for eighteen days on the field of Kuru, and many great warriors die. The earth trembles under the weight of the charging war elephants, chariots throw up clouds of dust obscuring the horizon, blood flows in streams, and every day there is occasion for profound grief for both parties. The dialogue (from the

Bhagavad Gita) between Arjunå and his counsellor and charioteer, Kresnå, to whom Arjunå turns in desperation at the prospect of having to kill blood relatives, takes place on the eve of the battle. In this dialogue, Kresnå teaches his student the duties of his *satriå* caste, which must take precedence over personal sentiments. The events which take place during the eighteen days, each of which are described in the epic, are full of tragedy. The old, honoured teachers from both sides go to their deaths, along with many young heroes, such as Bimå's son, Gatotkåcå, and Arjunå's sons, Irawan and Abimanyu. In the final part of the battle, Arjunå kills his half-brother, Karnå, and Suyudånå, the leader of the Koråwå, is killed by Bimå. The sounds of battle stop and a deep, ominous silence falls. The Pandåwå are victorious, but at the cost of all happiness and energy in their lives. The old power is broken, and Yudistirå, the eldest of the Pandåwå, accepts the reins of government and reigns over Astinå as a good and pious king.

After Kresnå's death, the Pandåwå decide to withdraw from the world and Parikesit, Arjunå's grandson, becomes king. The reign of Parikesit heralds the end of the purwå era on Java. He is seen as the ancestor of the Javanese kings, who therefore see themselves as descendants of the Pandåwå brothers. The story ends with the difficult journey of the Pandåwå to the Himalayas, to the divine mountain of Meru, where their souls ascend to heaven. In the *lakon* this episode is left out, and the Pandåwå disappear without a trace after the birth of Parikesit.

Page 138: King Kresná, 54 cm, 19th century, Cirebon, west Java. The extremely intelligent and composed King Kresná, incarnation of the god Wisnu, is depicted here at his apotheosis: he has a perfect royal appearance. His body is totally black, indicating complete spiritual strength and purity. The praise which this great king enjoyed everywhere is clear from the following passage: 'Kresná quickly left the kingdom of Wirata [...] and the great strength of the horses soon brought him to his destination, as if he had floated through the air. While the whole feast was prepared, which was of a kind only to be found in the *kraton* (palace) and consisted of six different flavours, Kresna arrived before the city. The resonance of the garantungs which welcomed him sounded deeply affectionate. He slowly rode past the banquet halls with his chariot. Those who wished to witness the arrival of the king made haste to the place of the spectacle, concerned that they would arrive too late. There were some who were still busy dressing their hair, but then the coils of hair came undone on the way. Others were still busy blackening their teeth, but because the party had arrived before they were ready, the teeth were half white and half black. [...] And those who were stringing flowers together arrived with the unfinished garlands in their hands. It was as if they wanted to pursue the king in order to show him the flowers. So, in their great haste, these women dropped their *kain* – which had come loose on the way – on the ground, concerned that they would arrive too late to see the king ride past. Because they climbed onto a scaffolding too hastily, it broke, and it unavoidably ended up looking like a scene of drunken revelry.'

History of the Ramayana and Mahabharata

The Indian epic Ramayana is known throughout South-East Asia. The Ramayana is attributed to the wise man Valmiki (Javanese *Walmiki*), according to legend a contemporary of Rámá himself. He lived during the Vedic age of the 12th to the 10th centuries BC. It is assumed that the 10th-century poet Yogiswara translated the Ramayana into *kakawin*, ancient Javanese poetry in Sanskrit metre on Java. It is probably the longest poem of the period: 2,774 verses.

The theme of the Mahabharata is the tragic conflict between two families of the Kuru line, descendants of the Bharátá, the Pandáwá and the Koráwá. The Mahabharata (Javanese *Mahabarátá*), the monumental epic of 90,000 verses, attained its present form in India in about 400 AD, and is said to be based on a war in the 9th century BC between two neighbouring Indian tribes, the Kuru and the Panchala. The author of the poem is said to be the sage Vyasa (Javanese *Abiásá*), the ancestor of both warring parties, the Pandawa and the Kaurava.

The earliest known Indonesian text is an extremely abridged version of eight *parvan* (Sanskrit for 'chapter') in Old Javanese prose. Each chapter may have been compiled at a different time, though it is almost certain that three *parvan* were codified in about 996 AD, at the behest of the east-Javanese King Dharmawangsa. About thirty years later, during the reign of King Airlangga, the poet Mpu Kanwá wrote the beautiful *kakawin* 'Arjuná Wiwáhá', about Arjuná's period of asceticism as a hermit, inspired by a certain episode from the Mahabharata. In 1157, Mpu Panuluh completed the *kakawin* 'Bharatayudha' (the war of the Bharatas), which had been started by Mpu Sedah under the patronage of King Jáyábáyá. This *kakawin* is about the final battle between the Pandawa and the Kaurava, which lasted eighteen days. The Mahabharata has been a source of inspiration for Javanese and Balinese art ever since.

Over the centuries, the stories of Rámá and Mahabharata have been the subject of many wayang performances. It is known that at the beginning of the 1930s there were eighteen different *lakon* dealing with

Page 139: Prince Gatotkaca, 59.5 cm, early 19th century, Kraton Kasepuhan, Cirebon, west Java. Gatotkaca in the last phase of his life. His complete spiritual maturity, probably shortly before his death in the Bratayuda, the final battle, is shown by the colour of his body, which is all black. Striking is the golden mark on his cheek. The end of the 'curled lobster-claw' hairstyle is attached to the crown of his head, which is typical for the Pasisir style. The death of Gatotkaca on stage is very moving for the Javanese audience. People see him as a representative of the young men who heroically gave their lives in the fight for independence.

Left: Arjuná as a hermit, Mintárágá, 45.5 cm, 1993, Yogyakarta, central Java. Arjuná's legs are entangled in the plants, and his hair reaches to his knees. The puppet was made by wayang maker Ledjar in the style of Surakarta. The name Mintáragá, which Arjuná bears in this episode, is made up from 'wita-raga', meaning 'he from whom the passion has disappeared'.

'He had achieved the level of consciousness which is the reward for months of continual faithful worship of the divine. He sat there cross-legged, his gaze fixed straight ahead, always focussed on nothing but the tip of his nose. He had dissolved himself into nothingness, he heard and felt nothing, his heart was as pure as Infinity. The nymphs thought that they could easily seduce him with their beauty; if he were to look at her just once, then he would no longer be so aloof. They did not realise that contemplation is a source of great joy, compared to which even the pleasure of love pales into insignificance, like the height of a mere coconut seedling compared to the height of a mountain.' See also page 38.

material from the Råmå cycle. The Mahabharata cycle is generally assumed to take place later than the period related in the Råmå cycle. There are certain *lakon* that establish this chronological link between the Råmå and Pandåwå cycles, but there are also *lakon* in which Råmå and his followers are the contemporaries of the Pandåwå.

There are dozens of *lakon* in which the Mahabharata is the subject, but only a few are actually about the origins of the Pandåwå and Koråwå families and their final downfall as a result of the Bråtåyudå. Many *lakon* deal with certain parts of the story. They can thus be seen as elaborations of a certain theme or period, for example the upbringing of the Koråwå and Pandåwå princes. These *lakon* are called *lakon carangan*. Another type of *lakon*, the *lakon sempalan*, are new stories that were added to the repertoire later on. The characters featured in these *lakon* are from the original Mahabharata epos, but the narratives themselves have nothing to do with the tales from the Mahabharata.

Right: Bagong, 38 cm, 1960, Surakarta, central Java.
Profile of the puppet depicted on page 71.

Bibliography

Anderson, B.R.O'G. 1965. *Mythology and the Tolerance of the Javanese*. Ithaca, N.Y.

Boedihardjo 1922. Grepen uit de Wayang. In: *Djåwå* 1, March 1922.

Brandon, J.R. 1970. *On Thrones of Gold. Three Javanese Shadow Plays*. Cambridge, Mass.

Clara van Groenendaal, V.M. 1982. *Er zit een dalang achter de wayang*. Amsterdam.

Ditjen Kebudayaan Departemen P&K [1980]. *Ensiklopedi Wayang Purwa I*. Jakarta.

Djajasoebrata, A.M.L.R. 1967. *Java, Wayang Purwa. Schaduwtoneel en wereldbeeld*. Tentoonstellingsgids Museum voor Land en Volkenkunde. Rotterdam.

Hadisoeseno, H. 1955. Wayang and Education. In: *Education and Culture* No. 8, October.

Hardjowirogo, R. 1968. *Sedjarah wajang purwa*. Djakarta.

Hazeu, G.A.J. 1897. *Bijdrage tot de kennis van het Javaansche tooneel*. Thesis, Leiden.

Heins, Ernst 1973. *Wajang Kulit. Het schimmenspel van Java, Indonesië*. Amsterdam.

Holt, C. 1965. *Art in Indonesia. Continuities and Change*. Ithaca, N.Y.

Hooykaas, C. 1933. *Proza en Poëzie van Oud-Java*. Groningen-Batavia.

Knaud, J.M. 1981. *Tussen schemering en dageraad. Achtergronden van de Wajang-Poerwa*. Den Haag.

Leur, J.C. van 1955. *Indonesian Trade and Society*. The Hague.

Mangkoenagårå VII, P.A.A. 1933. Over de wajang-koelit (poerwå) in het algemeen en over de daarin voorkomende symbolische en mystieke elementen. In: *Djåwå* 13.

Maurenbrecher, E.W. 1939. *De Panakawan-figuren in de Cheribonse Wajang*. In: Djåwå 19, pp. 187-190.

Mellema, R.L. 1954. *Wayang Puppets; Carving, Colouring and Symbolism*. Transl. by Mantle Hood, Koninklijk Instituut voor de Tropen, Amsterdam.

Noto Soeroto 1931. *Wayangliederen*. The Hague.

Pigeaud, Th. 1938. *Javaansche Volksvertoningen*. Bijdrage tot de beschrijving van land en volk. Batavia.

Poerbatjaraka, R.Ng. 1940. *Pandji-verhalen onderling vergeleken*. Bandoeng.

Poerbatjaraka, R.Ng. & Hooykaas C. 1934. Bharata-Yuddha (translated from old Javanese). In: *Djåwå* 14, pp. 1-87.

Ras, J.J. 1976. *De schending van Soebadra*. Amsterdam.

Rassers, W.H. 1959. *Pañji, the Culture Hero. A Structural Study of Religion in Java*. The Hague.

Serrurier, L. 1896. *De Wayang poerwå, eene ethnologische studie*. Leyden.

Soehatmanto, R.M. 1966. Seni Wajang Kulit. In: *Dian* 1/XUV.

Ulbricht, H. 1970. *Wayang Purwa. Shadows of the Past*. Kuala Lumpur.

Veldhuisen-Djajasoebrata A. 1973. Wajang perdjuangan. In: *Spiegel Historiael* 8, No. 2, February.

Wassing, R.S. 1983. *De wereld van de Wayang*. Delft.

Index

Glossary

Pronunciation

u	*like English 'good'*
å	*long 'o', like English 'snow'*
ḍ	deeply resonant, non-dental 'd', like 'dodo'
ṭ	non-dental 't', like 'later'

blencong traditional wayang lamp

bokongan way of wearing a *kain* (loincloth), see page 47

ḍalang wayang puppeteer

doḍot royal dress, twice as large as a *kain* (loincloth)

gårå-gårå moment of confusion during the wayang performance when the balance in nature is disturbed

garuḍå mythical bird

garuḍå mungkur wing-formed ornament shaped like a *garuḍå*

gender metallophone, instrument from the *gamelan* orchestra

gunungan leaf-shaped wayang prop fulfilling various functions: a mountain, a palace, a forest, the ocean, etcetera

jaitan almond-shaped eye with slit pupil

jamang diadem

kain loincloth measuring c. 1.20 x 2.50 m

kain poleng woven fabric in white and black, attributed with magical power

kawi old Javanese language rooted in Sanskrit

kedelen 'like a soya bean', here referring to the pupil of an eye

kelir wayang screen

ketu headdress

koṭak wayang chest

kraton palace

lakon stage adaptations from wayang literature

liyepan see *jaitan*

makuta royal crown

någå mythical snake

natah to chisel a wayang puppet

ngruwat to ritually cleanse, purge

nyungging to paint wayang puppets

pakem handbook for dalang

pånåkawan (disformed) attendants of princes and main characters from the wayang

pancanaka the razor-sharp thumbnail with which Bimå kills his enemies

pandita priest

patih first minister, state governor

perampogan wayang prop representing an army

perang gagal the first battle in a wayang performance

perang kembang introduction to combats which lead to the decisive final battle

perjuangan fight or revolution

praba wing-shaped ornament worn on the back symbolizing a halo or nimbus

resi holy teacher

ruwatan wayang performance to ward off evil and cleanse the surroundings

sajen offering

suluk chanted metres rendering a certain mood

sumping ear ornament

supit urang hairstyle shaped 'like the claw of a lobster': an upward curl of hair combined with a smaller one on the forehead that curls backwards

telengan round eye with large pupil

topeng mask

topong low crown

triwikråmå change of form achieved by exertion of supernatural powers

Wali the holy bringers of Islam in Indonesia

wåndå physical expression of moods

From left to right: Heavenly nymph and three
princesses, 32 cm, 1930, Surakarta; 32 cm, 1930
Surakarta; 27 cm, 1900, Cirebon; 31 cm, 1900,
Yogyakarta. Nymphs are given as a bride to human
heroes as a reward for doing good deeds for the
gods. This nymph is wearing a bridal headdress and
bridal *kebaya*. As an inhabitant of heaven she is
entitled to wear shoes. A princess stands before her
dressed in the style of Surakarta with her hair in a
large knot, as is still common in the Surakarta
region. Behind her is an unmarried princess with
her hair hanging loose, in the style of Yogyakarta.
The princess furthest to the right is dressed in the
style of Surakarta.

Credits

Original wayang texts

Translated by Andrew May

Page 39, caption: Hooykaas 1933: 160
Page 73: Boedihardja 1922
Page 100, caption: Hooykaas 1933: 167
Page 110, caption: Poerbatjaraka and
Hooykaas 1934: 16
Page 123, caption: Poerbatjaraka and
Hooykaas 1934: 73
Page 136, caption: Poerbatjaraka and
Hooykaas 1934: 62-63
Page 137, caption: Poerbatjaraka and
Hooykaas 1934: 11
Page 141, caption: Hooykaas 1933: 160

Illustrations

MvVR Museum of Ethnology, Rotterdam,
The Netherlands
KITLV Royal Instute of Linguistics and
Anthropology, Leiden, The Netherlands

Front cover: MvVR 58880
Back cover: KITLV 3668
Page 1: MvVR 67097
Page 2-3: MvVR
Page 6: KITLV 3982
Page 8: KITLV 27760
Page 10: MvVR
Page 12: MvVR 21762
Page 13: MvVR 26093
Page 14-15: KITLV 27.764
Page 18-19: MvVR F2971/76 (Photo: K. Céphas)
Page 20-21: KITLV 12.034
Page 22: MvVR 47916
Page 25: MvVR
Page 26: MvVR 25369 and MvVR 25376
Page 27: MvVR 25346 and MvVR 25379
Page 28: MvVR

Page 32: MvVR
Page 33: MvVR
Page 34: MvVR
Page 38: MvVR 72335
Page 40 left: MvVR 12901
Page 40 right: private collection
Page 48: MvVR 58984
Page 50: MvVR 58965
Page 51: MvVR 57790
Page 52: MvVR 58855 (left) and
MvVR 58852 (right)
Page 53: MvVR 60831
Page 54: MvVR 58992
Page 55: private collection
Page 56: MvVR 58961
Page 57: MvVR 71923
Page 58: MvVR 57775
Page 59: MvVR 58963
Page 60/61: MvVR 57978
Page 62: MvVR 67097
Page 63: MvVR 52628
Page 64: MvVR 52628
Page 65: MvVR 52629
Page 68: (from left to right) MvVR 57657, MvVR
57653, MvVR 57645, MvVR 57649 and MvVR 57652
Page 71: MvVR 57653
Page 72: MvVR 68701 and MvVR 57960
Page 74/75: MvVR 56702 (left), MvVR 56490
(centre) and MvVR 57647 (right)
Page 78: MvVR 57054
Page 76: MvVR 49528
Page 79 above: MvVR 34401
Page 79 below: MvVR 34402
Page 80/81: MvVR
Page 88/89: MvVR
Page 90: KITLV 3668
Page 92: MvVR 57983 (left) and
MvVR 58857 (right)
Page 95: MvVR 58866
Page 96: MvVR 20946
Page 97: MvVR 52630
Page 98: KITLV 1802 (left) and
KITLV 1804 (right)

Page 99: KITLV 1785 (left) and KITLV 1766 (right)
Page 106: MvVR 65381
Page 107: MvVR 58958 (left) and
MvVR 58959 (right)
Page 108: MvVR 57949
Page 109: MvVR 65380
Page 111: MvVR 58854
Page 112: MvVR 34442
Page 113, above: MvVR 12905
Page 113, below: MvVR 56718
Page 115: private collection
Page 117: KITLV 1851 (left) and KITLV 1834 (right)
Page 118: KITLV 1830 (left) and KITLV 1862 (right)
Page 122: MvVR 12901
Page 124: MvVR 58073 (left) and
MvVR 58974 (right)
Page 129: MvVR 12887 (left) and
MvVR 9562 (right)
Page 130/131: MvVR 52631 (left) and
MvVR 56491 (right)
Page 134: MvVR 58928
Page 135: MvVR 58880
Page 138: private collection
Page 139: MvVR 58897
Page 140: MvVR 72336
Page 150/151: private collection